# The Courage to Speak Up

## Getting Your Hairballs Out

2013

Here's to a new life!

Katy Byrne

# The Courage to Speak Up

## Getting Your Hairballs Out

Katy Byrne

Cartoons by Steve Klein

Langmarc Publishing
Austin, Texas

# The Courage to Speak Up
## Getting Your Hairballs Out

**by Katy Byrne**
**Illustrator: Steve Klein**

Editor: Catherine Hart
Cover Artist and Illustrator: Steve Klein
Cover Graphics: Michael Qualben



First Printing: 2007
Revision Printing: 2012
Printed in the United States of America



Published by
LangMarc Publishing
P.O. Box 90488
Austin, Texas 78709
www.langmarc.com

Library of Congress Control No. in process
ISBN: 978-1-880292-98-3

# Dedication

This book is dedicated to animal rights. The creatures of this world (individuals of another species) who have taught me how to forgive, about kindness, humor, letting go, faith, and flexibility. Let us respect and learn from them.

Animals are beyond us in their ability to show unconditional regard even without words. Have you ever felt judged by your dog wagging his tail at the door or your cat purring? They are the voiceless ones, yet they love unconditionally. They rely on our voices for their safety and protection.

# Table of Contents

**To contact Katy Byrne**

email her at KatyByrne@aol.com
www.KatyByrne.com
www.conversationswithKaty.com
707-548-8982

# Preface

As much as I believe that conversation can change the world, both personally and politically, I have to admit I have always grappled with it myself. How do you say things you would rather not say? What if you speak and the other person makes you feel like you're crazy? When you don't speak, what are the consequences? Separation, conflict, addictions, violence, paranoia, sore throats, constipation, backstabbing, (otherwise known as word of mouth). These are just a few of the possible results if we don't speak up.

My cat knew how to get his hairballs out better than I did. By watching him, I learned to speak up instead of stuffing what was stuck inside. I lost one hundred pounds, and I started journal writing, which became a column in a newspaper and then this book.

Hairballs are a lot like getting out what you have to say even when your stomach is turning—spitting it out, hacking, sounding like a death rattle or boots pouncing through a mud puddle, hairballs can be messy, mixed up, irrational, complaining, excited, jagged or disorganized, laying gummy on the ground.

To clarify: I don't encourage dumping on people. I do think we live in a world that discourages our truth, and the result is one big world full of hairballs. Have I spoken up enough about the importance of speaking up?

I guess this book should have been called *The Difficulty of Speaking Up* because good conversation is an act of bravery. I have discovered in my own life and in talking to people that communication takes courage. That's why we don't do it. The divorce rate is high, wars rage and people don't create enough solutions to the world's problems because that would require us to have the kind of continual dialogue that creates change.

We hesitate to state our convictions. Why? Many clients and friends don't speak up because they struggle to withstand criticism without collapsing inside or blaming themselves. Others have a defensive structure of shaming, conflict and self-doubt. So, we are somewhat like the national guard – keeping each other separate.

The "fight or flight" instinct can be stronger than dealing with uncomfortable feelings. It's simply scary to be seen, heard or to be vulnerable. I've had friends disappear after ten years of closeness and not even want to talk about why. I've been lectured to and gotten advice (not wanted), been judged or misunderstood. Sometimes communication is one big hairball.

I have an acquaintance who can't speak to her daughter. One shuts down, the other slams doors and gets stomachaches instead of talking. They long to be close but who is going to start? And these are just brief examples of a larger problem.

Even having a conversation within myself can be confrontational. I might learn something I'm afraid to know. In *Silencing the Self* Dana Jack said, "To take one's feelings seriously, to acknowledge and consider them, pulls one beyond the confines of ordinary thought. Authentic feelings can also require action by making a person too aware, too unhappy to remain within the status quo." Knowing how we really feel sometimes requires movement. Connecting to our longings and wishes can be the beginning of a revolution, personal and collective change.

When I stopped eating compulsively and listened to the parts (voices) in my head, it was sheer anguish to hear the small child inside who was desperate for love. It wasn't easy to let my angry self scream out in a safe place. Over the years I had allowed myself to be abused, both by myself and others. Yes, I wanted to stuff down those hairballs.

But, who can speak up for unfairness and for the voiceless ones (children, prisoners, women in subhuman conditions, the elderly, animals, etc.) better than those of us with a voice?

Speaking up is not so easy. To speak up, we need to reveal our own deepest longings and experiences and to drop walls.

Dana Jack says: "Depressed women are afraid that if they try to be themselves they will lose their marriages." She describes one woman as saying: "If I do tell him how I'm feeling about something I'm shot down." Notice the wording *shot,* like a gun.

For men the issue is also fear as Terrence Real describes in *I Don't Want to Talk About It:*

> "...to the degree to which a man learns to 'be strong' and to devalue weakness, his compassion towards frailty not just in himself but also in those around him may be limited or condescending. In this and many other ways, the loss of expressivity and the loss of vulnerability inevitably lead to diminished connection with others...."

Disclosure is not valued in our society. Yet opening up is a binding force in marriages and in heartfelt communities. Why can't we bridge gaps, work through differences, or even talk to ourselves effectively? Wouldn't resolutions to the world's problems emerge from real dialogues?

Talking to each other in a way that creates long-lasting change is difficult, too, because blaming is our strongest impulse. (It comes from the limbic brain – the protective instinct to strike out.) It's the messy hairball running rampant in the world. Fighting is the result.

I'm not without fault here either. It's simply easier to judge others than to take responsibility for my life. Sometimes there is evil or unfairness and it's necessary to get angry or set a boundary, and sometimes we imagine that too many problems are our entire fault, so what to do?

We speak readily about powers over us, betraying us, or taking our freedom but what is at the murky bottom of this? Besides huge systems bullying us or pushing us down, there is also the dark place we don't admit. We don't ask for what we want because we're ashamed, despairing, or giving up. Our hurt has been lost in learned helplessness. Our anger and frustration is useful only when directed towards solutions.

Between shame and blame, my psyche is always ready to pounce on me. "Aha, see, you are too emotional, too outspoken, not articulate, not enough or too much." Will I lose my job? A friend? I guess I'll let it go." But, where does "it" go? Lost connections, eating more cookies, failing health, fewer alliances?

Brenee Brown says in *The Gift of Imperfection*, "Shame loses power when it is spoken…it is human nature to want to feel worthy of love and belonging. When we experience shame we feel disconnected and desperate for worthiness; full of shame or fear of shame, we are more likely to engage in self destructive behaviors or to attack or shame others."

Sometimes I feel as if I have to breathe into my chest and tell myself I deserve to have my say. I used to feel frightened to talk to my boss. Would I find the courage to tell her I felt hurt? Would I be able to identify my intention and needs? I wanted to say, "Can we show more respect for each other?" But, it's hard being naked in front of the world.

If emotions and needs stay buried and aren't heard, how can they be healed? If I don't feel my own pain, how can I build compassion or even know what I need? Ideally, with safe witnesses I find relief for my soul.

Crime and violence is in part a result of repressed and wounded people who were never heard. How do we heal despair? We share it. Then another kind of fire emerges, the kind that cares. Our inner rage at allowing ourselves to be put down may need to be felt.

John Backman said in *The Dialogue Venture:* "With the challenges we face as human beings, this pursuit of dialogue is important. The future of our marriages, of our churches, even of the planet may depend on it. If we cannot talk openly and in a civil manner about family conflict or matters of faith, let alone climate change or nuclear armament, how can we ever overcome the problems that threaten us all?"

People are lonely with the constant use of machines. We long for connection, intimacy, comfort and aliveness. I run to my computer, but it doesn't replace connection. There is no way a machine can feel or understand. Technology is full of black and white thinking.

Finally, as a prelude to the many hairballs to come in this book, I have to add that the political arena is a swirling of argument, full of power struggles and put downs. We don't have to feel helpless or at a loss for what to do. Humans need the courage to speak up at every opportunity, in small, private or large arenas. That might mean dropping the fear of embarrassment or imperfection. In particular, if we could tell our personal stories as well as retracing statistics and offering solutions, we might have a basis for reform.

The most successful movements in our history have come from people who cried out for a new vision, from deep personal truth and conviction. At the roots of change are real people needing to be heard. The personal is political.

Respectful dialogue, with enough time to earn trust, builds bridges. Some people think the problems are too big or argue that talking isn't going anywhere; (we do have to "do "something,) but just doing is not enough. What we have not done is come together and put our cards on the table. It is only from brainstorming, sharing and choosing new ways to live that we unify and become proactive in large enough numbers to empower us.

With so much ingenuity, brilliance, creativity, life force, and community, we could be creating a world that is fair for all. At this pivotal point in history can we connect in conversations, share our grief and create solutions for a world in trouble?

**In the beginning was the word.**

*—Katy Byrne*

# ACKNOWLEDGMENTS

With special thanks to my parents for taking me through the first half of my life; my brother Lee Zwettler for loving me unconditionally and always making me chuckle; my partner, Steve Klein, for his patience, heart, and artistry with the "toons."

Deep gratitude goes to Fyrne Rudorf, who typed and edited with infinite humor, wisdom, and helpfulness; Catherine Hart for her brilliant editing; Gabriel Constans, my agent, for his steadfast belief in me; to Lois and Mike Qualben at LangMarc Publishing for their faith in me, Rose Byrne for her constant and never wavering administrative and personal support. To Richard Lardner for insisting that I not drop the ball on this idea and even typing for me into the night.

To Kate Yates for continuing to inspire the wild woman in me. And, with deep gratitude to *Sonoma County Women's Voices* newspaper and *The Sun News* who have supported my hairballs columns for years. And to all the dear friends, family, and helpers who worked like ants to hold me up when I wanted to crumble. It is because of these people, the ones who have passed the ball, back and forth, that I was able to complete this book and have some fun doing it. I hope you know who you are. Thank you all from the bottom of my heart.

And, of course, to my darling cats who have kept the hairball concept going: the ones I live with now—Aristotle, Freud, Marilyn—and the ones who have come before and gone, like my most precious Einstein. A last good-bye to Harold and Gretchen, who taught me most how to love. Finally a humble bow to my new, darling, rescue pooch Toodles, who makes me smile every day.

# Introduction

> *Only kind, deep listening and loving speech can help restore communication and remove wrong perceptions, the foundation of all hatred, violence, and terrorism.*
>
> Thich Nhat Hanh
> *Calming The Fearful Mind*

In a world that shames us for being honest, getting out our hairballs can be painful, but exhilarating and transforming. Constant emotional stuffing causes congestion of body and soul. At least cats cough up the hairball when it gets stuck. Not us. It's the fear of real conversation that is a major problem in our lives and our world. But it takes learning to express who we really are if we want the intimacy we crave in our relationships and world peace.

*The Courage to Speak Up* is about talking to each other and discovering the roots of our feelings, thoughts, and actions so that we can connect in understanding of our diversity and common bonds.

*Getting Your Hairballs Out* is not about spitting out whatever comes to mind. They are not about dumping your demons and purging on anyone who is in your way. Hairballs help you identify your own needs and feelings at the deepest levels, and then connect in conversation with those you love (and those you don't). It's about getting access to the life we've choked down—it needs to come out.

Keeping a personal journal or speaking out can be cathartic, insightful, and revitalizing.

Why have so many balls in the air and be all balled up when you can change that through conversation with yourself and others? As a world, we are now at a primitive stage of communication. The hairball reflects some of the dark side we hold in, but it shows up in war and conflict. Isn't it time we took a look at it? It's time to get on the ball.

Whether you choose to speak through journaling, correspondence, through hand movements or making sounds, by phone, or in person—for health and happiness, let your hairballs roll!

This book holds my hairballs in various settings. I support you in speaking up about yours.

# Chapter One

## Einstein, the Hairball and Me

# Why I Write Hairballs

## It is My Contention That Conversation Can Change the World

*In spite of deep-seated craving for love, almost everything else is considered to be more important than love: success, prestige, money, power – almost all our energy is used for the learning of how to achieve these aims, and almost none to learn the art of loving.*

Erich Fromm
*The Art of Loving*

Sitting one winter night feeling frustrated, lost, and confused, I looked over at my cat Einstein blurting out a hairball. He dropped it neatly in a spot on the corner of my desk, arched his back, stretched some more, then circled around, finding his perfect perch atop my warm computer. He looked so relieved as he purred. I said, "Einstein, you're a genius!" In that moment, I began to type and get out what was bothering me. My "dear diaries" became this book.

As I wrote I thought: How can cats relax so well when I tend to worry and hold things in? Could my cat teach me something about living comfortably? Isn't it actually unkind to ourselves to always fear conflict and stuff our truth? I mean, hairballs are messy by their very nature.

Einstein was such a grounding force for me because his upsets were always followed by complete calm. He could even get into a brawl, then settle down and become friends with his enemies. He didn't hold grudges, and he loved me no matter what. So, if he could let it all hang out, express what he needed to, and then curl up in my arms—why can't we humans do that?

Each of us has feelings and needs stuffed inside that make us sick, tired, depressed, and lonely. I'm not saying we should run around, getting it all out, crying "Bleak!" But, with the right tools and intentions, I think "coughing up" clears things.

It takes guts to get out what's bugging us. It takes courage to tell the truth and admit our longings. It's an ultimate act of bravery to take the ball and run with it—to commit to a life of meaning and passion.

Seeing the peacefulness it brought Einstein to get out the congestion in his gut and throat (the hairball) was a precious gift.

I saw the power of talk and journaling when, through my writing and revealing myself with safe people, I was able to recover from an eating disorder. Before that, I could not stop eating. I felt ugly and fat. I got through that horror show by going deep into my feelings and getting them out. And, by clinging to my diary, I touched yearnings and learned to follow them instead of chasing éclairs.

This book is about love and why it's so difficult to find. It's what we want more than anything, but the hardest to get. By mustering the courage to keep talking, we bridge gaps. So many marriages end because one or both people couldn't communicate. Dialogue helps us connect, brings us closer. The loss that occurs when relationships end or disappear into the black hole is often never forgotten, children not speaking to families, friendships lost, or war. If we can't drop walls between us or express ourselves completely, we never get the hairball out. Love doesn't go away; it stays in the body. The heart knows. The soul knows.

I've been in and out of therapy, seminars, workshops, meditation retreats, and twelve-step programs. I became a therapist in a quest for truth and fulfillment. I started writing in order to hear myself. All this has helped. I've learned to feel pain, to be myself with less shame or fear of being judged. I am more comfortable in social settings just being myself. I got thin and I dropped 100 pounds when I started speaking up.

Now, looking back on 25 years both as a therapist and client, I think something new is needed. We need a world in which community cares, in which we support each other's triumphs, grief, and common fears. Healing requires self-expression, with agreements from willing participants.

We speak of God a lot these days, but isn't God love? How loving are we? How often do we judge, bolt, or blame? We need a witness for our sorrow and excitement. We need to trust that we can share our deepest selves, not in secret, in a small room, but to say to the world without shame, "This is who I am."

Telling the truth often terrifies me. I used to stop doing it because I thought it wouldn't help matters and would rock the boat. "Why bother? It's not worth it." These were typical excuses I gave myself for withdrawing from others. But in the second half of life, in particular, we face the possibility of dying before we ever felt alive. We need to be able to dialogue safely with our neighbors and have, as its primary intention, listening with no need to fix or judge. So often I find if I can sit down with someone after we've disliked each other, we're surprised as our sincere fears unfold to discover compassion and even humor.

If the enraged male could sob in the lap of another John Wayne, if the single mother of three could tell her community of the loneliness of her nights and of her struggles, if we each felt less embarrassed to share, with so many sorrows and challenges facing us all, we might have a different world.

It is my contention that conversation can change the world. Dialogue creates connection and clarity. It takes time and sorting, but talking to each other is a bridge needed more than ever in these trying times.

The hairball concept was a gift from my cat. I saw the relief and peacefulness it brings as I watched him get out the congestion sitting in his gut and throat.

It is not an easy road; if it were, we would all be doing it. There are no guarantees when we talk to each other, get out our hairballs honestly, and ask for what we need. But the irony is, there's really only one road to choose: tell the truth or die, because holding in the hairball is an insidious death, like constipation slowly killing you. Voice helps relieve tension, tightness, excess weight, and addictions. Voice helps identify what hurts and excites us, and so does writing. It is a life of risk, a life of deliberate creation to say and to admit what you feel at the most vulnerable level and to express your sincere needs and believe you deserve to have them met.

There are so many fears that stop us from speaking up, and the first step is admitting those to ourselves. Afraid of rejection, shame, blame or conflict, it takes courage to speak up.

I do not advocate impulsive speaking, even while having a hairball. I believe in pondering, preparing, meditating, and knowing what really matters. If you are caring, even if you're angry but your intention is good, things will begin to flow. By getting the ball rolling through speech or writing, you can hear and feel more vividly your deepest wishes so that you can thrive. Then take the ball and run with it.

As Henry Thoreau said, "In wildness is the preservation of the world." It is time to speak up.

## HAIRBALLS FOR THE READER

What changes do you most wish for in your life?

What fears or beliefs stop you from going for it?

# Things Left Unsaid

## The Result of Not Speaking Up

*When dialogue dies, as it can with either person's failure to speak, to hear, or to acknowledge the other, then part of the self also dies.*

Dana Crowley Jack
*Silencing the Self*

Things unsaid can sever relationships. The things I never said walk with me each day like my shadow, waking me up at night when I most want to forget. I believe separation and war come from something deep inside that's unexpressed.

I write about needing to get the hairball out because I learned from my cat that it's important to express what's bothering you. The times I didn't get it out, didn't say what mattered to me more than anything, and the times I held my breath have greatly affected my life and relationships. When I didn't say what hurt and scared me and what I needed, I lost a little of my life force, my soul and creativity—the umbilical cord to my power.

The things you stuff, that you don't say, can dull your inner flame. They can turn to lethargy, resentments, judgments, and unspoken fears that make you want to run and not participate. Things unsaid turn to poison.

But sometimes we create havoc with the things we do say. We cause so much upset we want to bolt. So what can we do? Learn to skillfully say what matters and tolerate hearing unpleasant feedback. Patient listening and saying things to others in a way that's not wounding is just as important as being heard.

The time I most wrestled with stuffed feelings was when my mother was dying. She had emphysema. She was a feisty woman, and I loved her more than myself. I loved our vibrant conversations, her honesty and compassion, and I loved her humor.

But how do you tell the truth to a sick, depressed, angry, old person? When she knew she was dying, she was locked to a breathing machine and couldn't easily leave the house. I flew to visit her and spent several days there. As I packed to leave, she did something she'd never done before: she begged me to stay. She said, "I'm afraid, I need you. I've never asked you for anything before; please stay."

I knew my mom and I were much too merged and that she'd smothered me as a kid. I'd learned in therapy about boundaries, and I decided I needed to not be codependent. I was drained and I wanted to take care of myself. I thought I was doing the right thing by leaving, by not blurting out too much and hurting her feelings, making matters worse. So I stuffed everything. I couldn't breathe for all the hair in my throat and I left. I flew home. She died.

That was when I first learned about the horror and loss that comes with keeping words inside. I'd lost a connection because I hadn't been able to say what I needed. I wailed alone. Before that, even with all my years in therapy, it had never occurred to me that holding in my hairball would mean so much pain.

She died alone, and my most fragile feelings and wishes stayed in my throat. Now I believe having too many limits separates us and that boundaries are a substitute for soul. Sometimes our cherished boundaries become a substitute for the depth of soul it takes to reach out. I think we sometimes push people away, just when we most want to connect. And often we blame instead of dropping down into our most core communication. How do I know when I'm at my deepest truth? I usually feel embarrassed.

I wish more than anything that I'd let it out. I long, still, in every cell of my being, to say to her:

> Dearest Mom, if you can hear me now, I want you to know, more than anything, I was afraid. I was terrified that you wouldn't listen, that you couldn't calm down and quit raging at me. I needed you to understand that I didn't want to leave but I was frozen, scared of making it worse, saying the wrong thing, having a fight—so I said nothing. So now, forever between us is this gulf—a cliff to fall off with no bridge. I was scared of listening to your anger and your monologues, afraid of your fury, your criticisms. But most of all, I just wanted you to hear my needs, to listen to me, too.
>
> I couldn't say any of this; I didn't know how to ask you for what I so desperately wanted. I was

afraid I'd become exhausted and die, too. I couldn't find a way to talk to you: about death, about dad being gone, about our relationship. I didn't know how to be vulnerable, speak of my fear and needs. The only thing I knew was to stuff everything inside, keep it in. I offer you now, much too late, this courageous conversation.

## HAIRBALLS FOR THE READER

What have you left unsaid and/or to whom?

What communications will you regret if you don't complete them before you die?

What do you fear in telling your truth?

What has not speaking up cost you?

Can you say what you feel responsibly, without blaming?

## Note to My Daughter Katy

(Last poem written to Katy from her mother, Lea,
just before she died))

Darling, since I now am deep in the prime of life—
Old enough by all means to know seems from is—
I would pass my knowledge onto you, my darling,
And tell you exactly what life really is.

I would like to tell you how to take life's palette,
Color it with friendship, love, dancing, and grace.
How to be an artist who sketched happiness
With indelible courage, which none could erase.

If I knew the answers (or, indeed, the questions)
To the worldly riddle I would tell you all.
As it is, I'll just say, "try to keep your nose clean,
Eat right, brush your teeth and watch the bouncing
ball."

Lea

Mom and Dad

My brother, Lee, and Me

# Food and the Hunger for Love

*Food and love... if we haven't been loved well, recognized, understood... we lower our expectations.... We stop asking for what we need. We stop showing the places that hurt or need comfort. We stop expecting to be met....*

Geneen Roth
*When Food is Love*

I didn't know that speaking up would cause me to lose weight. I cry when I talk about my eating disorder. I sometimes explode with grief for the years I suffered, even though I've been free for twenty-five years now. I never think about food anymore: I eat, don't eat, no big deal. But for so long, shame, chronic confusion and longing for a normal life penetrated my pores, my cells. I thought compulsively about food, wanting it to go away, hating myself, trying things that didn't work.

There was never a time I wasn't thinking about food: getting it, hiding it, swallowing it, being seen eating it. Food followed me like a shadow.

I couldn't quit eating; eating was my life. Nobody understands this disorder unless they've had it. It's like living in hell and being crucified every day. Every time I ate, I felt anguish from over stuffing myself, yet I was never full inside.

Talking with a client recently, I became overwhelmed with tears and shock. I realized that my recovery was a miracle. I'd been walking through a dark jungle for so many lonely years. Now I can look back and feel free of that psychic drain, that constant obsession.

Sure, I still watch the ten pounds come and go. I go from a size eight to a size eleven (depending on intimacy issues, sorrow, or anxiety), but I don't worry that food is my life or that it'll gobble me up. My concerns about it now are centered on pleasure, health, or seeing what's going on with me emotionally since my body always gives me a clue when I'm painfully full or eating a lot of junk. It's my compass. My body tells me what I need to look at and move through.

I tried everything: diets, nutritionists, exercise, prayer, and twelve-step programs. They all helped, but the breakthrough came when I finally ran to a therapist friend and, in desperation, threw myself on her floor and let out my feelings. I cried, sobbed, screamed, and got my deepest hairball out: I found a little girl in me who needed care, craved affection, and thought love was in the cupboards and grocery stores.

I remember the day I stood with the fridge door open and cried, staring inside. I talked to my inner kid that day before devouring the food. I said, "What is it you really want? I won't beat you up any more for it, just talk to me." She said, "I want food, get me chocolate-covered malt balls, wheat thins, donuts, and pizza." I said, "Okay. I'll get them for you, but will that make you feel better? What is it you really need?" That was the beginning of the change. She said, "I don't want to be bloated and sick. I need to be soothed. I want to be loved in order to feel full." I said, "What would do that for you?"

That's where my story begins. I felt stupid standing at the fridge talking to myself, but that was my way of getting the hairball out.

## HAIRBALLS FOR THE READER

What habits do you use to block yourself from your true feelings?

What do your addictions numb out? (Include work, TV, etc.)

What activities and thoughts help you to feel most full in your life?

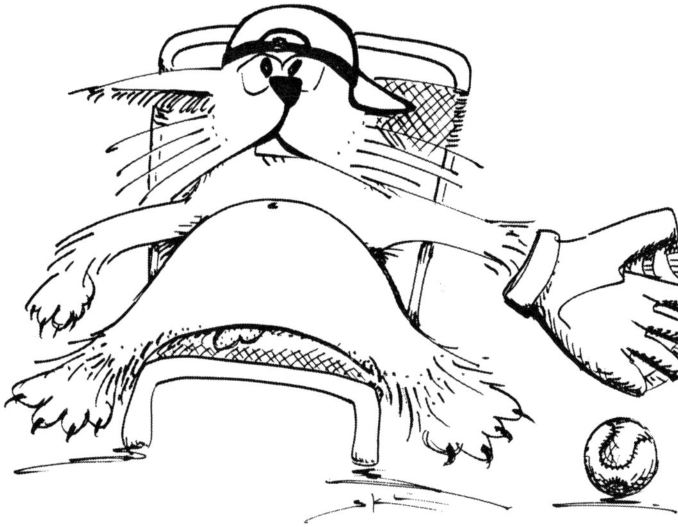

# Cojones On Dad

*Sons don't want their fathers' balls; they want their hearts. And for many, the heart of a father is a difficult item to come by.*

Terrence Real
*I Don't Want to Talk About It*

My father was passive, shut down a lot. He held things in, giving him ulcers and a bad back. I think that's where I get my built-in anxiety about making changes and speaking up. Fathers can teach their kids to assert themselves, to dream, to mobilize their talents in the world.

Don't get me wrong, I worshipped my father. But, growing up I learned that being strong meant being shut down and silent. I internalized a father who was sullen, ghostly, not quite there. I worshipped and adored my dad. It wasn't until late in life I realized he was very shy. I missed sharing his thoughts and emotions.

What would life have been if I'd had a father who spent time with me, taught me things, took me places?

Maybe having a stronger dad would have helped me feel an internal support when I'm challenged. Instead, I'm afraid I'll say the wrong thing or that I'll make a decision that's disastrous. I'm prone to depression.

The men in my family were absent. I was thinking about my brother Billy's death today, and I just couldn't deal with the fact that I never really knew my own brother. My parents put Billy in a home when he was small because he had Down's syndrome.

I guess in those days they didn't know what else to do. But I'm haunted! How sad that someone of my own blood was so separate from me.

Ironically, the man I admire most is the guy who took care of my developmentally disabled brother, not even a family kin. Now that took balls. He was the most generous and least self-centered person involved with Billy. He knew how to care. It seems odd to be learning so much now from John Sanders.

Though he had a wife, a job, and three children of his own, John took care of Billy when he could and spent time with him every week for years. He brought him to his home for holidays and enjoyed seeing Billy play with his own kids. John loved Billy. They laughed and they were friends. When Billy died of a brain tumor, John asked me repeatedly not to blame anyone. He understood why Mom and Dad couldn't keep Billy at home.

The funny thing is, Billy was the happiest person in our family, always optimistic and friendly. Perhaps Down's syndrome helped him live in the moment. He was grateful for everything.

Anyway, the grief has hit me hard, and I can't figure out exactly what's at the bottom of it. Is it because John Sanders is the way I really want to be? I am so moved by his nonjudgmental and giving nature. Is it the accumulation of all the losses of my life that would be just too much to feel? Do I miss my family?

John Sanders didn't seem to need my brother to be anything but himself. Billy could not chat at all, let alone get a hairball out, and it didn't matter. No words, no hairballs were ever needed between them, but there was love.

What if I had had a dad who was demonstrative? I adored him, but he never took me to the ball game, never asked me how I felt.

Why am I most sad tonight? I never knew one of my own brothers. My dad didn't open up much. Billy was a secret for many years. When Mom told me Billy was one of her children, I was already 21 years old. She had so much guilt, she sobbed.

The question this grief brings up for me is: How important is generosity of spirit and service to others? When to be selfish and when to give? I sit with this hairball tonight.

### HAIRBALLS FOR THE READER

Do you feel you have a strong "dad" inside that gives you the power to express yourself or stay grounded and compassionate and take action in the world? How might you acquire that strength?

What is one courageous thing in your family that you wish you could express or do? Describe yourself doing just that.

# Swallowing

*I didn't know that eating a meal was an act of kindness and would give my body the fuel it needed to think clearly, move fluidly....*

Geneen Roth
*When Food is Love*

I'm grateful I don't eat compulsively anymore, but I need to get this hairball out. Everyone is obsessed with weight loss these days, as though a carbohydrate is as evil as a terrorist. The media decides what's coming next, and we follow like lambs. Cigarettes are out, high heels are in, hairy armpits had their day. Now being weak and anorexic is the thing.

All this effort put into trying to be "perfect" is where the money is. But what is the bottom line on big bottoms really? Are they so bad? I'm tired of running after the next popular version of what to be. In my early years, Marilyn Monroe was in, and women with tiny breasts were ashamed of themselves. Then when lesbians started coming out of the closet, suddenly flat chests were a turn-on. When Barbie dolls became the ideal, we all ate as little as possible and wobbled around on four-inch heels, trying to feel powerful. What's this about?

Is it that some men want small women in order to feel big? And, why do we go along? Many guys are discovering that tiny women are not any more gentle than the rest of us. Tough divorce suits and the most rugged battles of the sexes happen just as often with petite women as with larger ones. Whatever our size, the bottom line for most women is that we want to be respected. Unfortunately, we rarely even offer that to each other.

I am sick and tired of face-lifting, hair-coloring, boring "ab" workouts, and applying botulism (better known as Botox) to my brows. I want to do what I enjoy and have my voice.

I wonder why women don't get together on this. We still seem to have a primitive instinct—nails out, claws dug in—to fight each other for the man or go full balls for the job promotion. Isn't it time we pursue new values like cooperation, respect, mutual support, and validating each other's strengths?

What if TV talk shows were about women's beauty in all sizes and conditions: large, lost, older, imperfect, or disabled; or about being totally loved and cherished by their husbands and friends? What if we were strong and vigorous instead of trying to be slim and imperceptible, starving ourselves while walking on stilts? Could we give each other respect all the time? Suppose women in powerful positions used their influence to support each other and important issues like access to affordable housing, how to help us work in jobs we love, or appreciating women's different sizes and shapes?

There is a desperate need for females to get involved in politics. There is a crying hole where women's voices should speak.

How can we stop trying to model ourselves after media images and begin empowering each other?

## HAIRBALLS FOR THE READER

How can you quit comparing yourself to media images?

What would make you feel more powerful?

How can you support other women more?

# Chapter Two

## Therapy and the Wounded Healer

# What's Up With Therapy?

## Working Through Blocks and Old Habits

*While some marriages end because of overt differences, many wither because couples never develop a way to bring up issues and successfully resolve them.*

Joshua Coleman, Ph.D.
*The Marriage Makeover*

Tonight I find myself wondering: How do we change? What makes it possible to break through old patterns? After years of being in therapy and a therapist myself, I continue to question: Why go to therapy? Is it even necessary? How do you know if you are being helped? How many times have I felt that it may not go anywhere at all? I can even remember being wounded as a client by getting bad advice or being patronized, which set me back.

I've been in and out of counseling, seminars, meditation retreats, and twelve-step programs all my life. I became a therapist in a quest for fulfillment. They've all helped in different ways. I've learned to feel emotions and be myself with less fear of being judged. I'm better at believing I'm okay and more comfortable in social settings. But, it isn't an end to my problems or moods. There is still work to do; there's always more to uncover, to allow myself to be fully human.

Having spent most of my life thinking about these issues, it reaffirms that good therapy is focused on the client because each person's victory is different. Some people find a spiritual way to serenity; others discover Prozac;™ many get breakthroughs in relationships and learning to love. Sometimes, prayer has brought miracles into my life. Sometimes my friends are most helpful if they don't shame me. I find out that even with my quirks, I can chuckle once again.

I've also discovered that once I know my true intent, my life begins to flow. I have been noticing this power: I see that every day thousands of cars line up on the road. They flow in and out of lanes and stop signs with very few accidents (compared to the number of people out there). The thing that amazes me is this: they get where they are going because they really want to. When you think of it, there are people out there in those cars who are zombied out on drugs, in the middle of domestic violence, folks who have just lost a loved one, people with kids, rage, radical politicians, psychos, comedians, and on and on. Yet, they get where they want to go. Really, sit for a minute and think of the enormity of this. This is the power of intention.

So, I ask myself, "What is mental health?" Looking back on 25 years, both as a therapist and as a client, I think getting out feelings with someone you trust is as important as getting clear on what you want; that is, establishing goals for yourself, not begrudging others, but being responsible for your own life. Being able to tolerate frustration and doubt while building supportive self-talk and continuing to take little steps forward so you can hold your head high and laugh at the absurdity of it all, that's important, too.

Staying stuck in therapy can be the biggest problem of all, and women especially have a tendency to ruminate on their emotions, messing in the hairball, poking around in the problem, questioning how it got on the rug, cleaning and complaining for days, even when solutions are available.

Thank God, I have had some tools and transformations. When I recovered from my eating disorder, it was a living hell. I had to struggle every day with the part of me that was lonely and looking for food in order to feel loved. I remember one night, armpit leaning into the open freezer door, staring at the ice cream and crying, talking to some inner, fragile child inside me. Talking to my therapist, I sobbed when I realized that what I really wanted was not three pizzas. The food was, in fact, a way to beat myself up, harm myself.

I will never forget the night when I was able to chat with my internal, starving kid and calm her; that was a turning point. I was jubilant and so full inside that I was able to take a bath, instead of eating, and get into bed with a great book instead of bread and butter. Instead of stuffing (the hairball), I was able to deeply relax and self-soothe. I was beginning to believe that I was entitled to a life of love, not of self-criticism and harm. This was an entire rearranging of my inner world.

I continue to struggle with sorrow at times, but a real life has many feelings, and I find that the people who like me really help. Because I tell them the truth, I am comforted and not condemned. These precious relationships have not been without squabbles or strife, but as one of my friends, Sara, says with a little Mona Lisa smile, "my friends love me the way I am because they know me, all of me." If Shakespeare, Thoreau, or Bette Midler had tried to be someone they weren't, what kind of world would this be? Being comfortable in one's own skin requires acceptance of oneself and others.

It is difficult today, staring into this computer, pulling at the curls around my earlobe, with a big question mark on my forehead. What does cause wonderful breakthroughs? Some of it is mystery. I scratch my scalp. Yeah, I have seen some miracles. I witnessed clients, sometimes the ones I least expected, have major transformations because they found their own way, even while resisting. What do I really think works in therapy? Learning, like the Buddhists, to accept some suffering, coupled with finding places to get support and discover solutions. And, shame is a killer. You've got to tell the internal critic to take a hike.

Moving ahead in life takes persistence. David Reynolds, who studied Japanese counseling, talks in *Constructive Living* about taking action and then processing the inevitable feelings afterwards. People have many strengths inside that need to be encouraged (that is why courage is a part of it). Too often in therapy we are "pathologized" instead of validated for our abilities. The great leaders in history had vision and in spite of all the sand traps, their balls landed where they intended them to go. Heroes are brave; instead of ruminating over the mess, they see possibilities, dreams, wishes; the way things could be.

Through helplessness or defeat, like focusing on the golf ball that is lost in the field or stuck in a sand pit and cannot be retrieved, we stay out of the game. This tendency, to stare into the black hole, is disempowering and dissipates energy. Sometimes speaking out loud and getting rid of the hairball gets false beliefs off your chest. In order to stop hitting your head against a wall, sometimes you need a safe place, a space in which there is agreement to vent. It's like driving; clear the fog off a windshield so you can see where you want to go.

In the end, good therapy can help us have relationships. You know, in these times, everyone is hassled and under stress. We need to come to the table with the desire to co-create, making clear requests instead of blaming; otherwise the entire hairball starts to unravel. Attacking is historically destructive. Can you state your vision instead? Be responsible for your part in building it?

When it comes to being in counseling, be careful who you hire, and trust your own intuition. Therapists are only human and some are biased. Good counselors should be focused on mutually defined goals of therapy.

For mental health, we need a world in which community cares, in which we support each other's triumphs, share losses and common fears, drop competition and judging, and help each other reconstruct old beliefs. It's essential that we stop beating up on ourselves and each other. Know we are deserving and quit thinking the, "I'm not worthy, I'm not worthy" shtick.

We need to talk to each other without shame and create safety in listening, not just in the confinement of one small room with paid support. Being able to blurt out your truth and then formulate it into a wish enables you to contribute to making changes in the world.

After all these years, it's clear: enjoying the ball game of life seems to me to involve a safe place to speak up, self acceptance, the willingness to change, and your wildest wishes. When you're healing, you feel innocent, kinder, and more playful. Inner war ends, there is peace.

## HAIRBALLS FOR THE READER

What makes it difficult for you to move forward in your life? What has most helped you?

What are your experiences, thoughts, and feelings about therapy?

What are your deepest intentions in life?

# The Black Hole Hairball

## The Critic

*When someone we love or desire betrays us, we are submerged in an unwelcome torrent of change. It hurts to realize that someone has lied to us, broken an agreement or deserted us.*

John Amodeo, Ph.D.
*Love and Betrayal*

We need courage to speak up in small moments, when we feel put down. We also need to say "no" to our inner critic. We terrorize ourselves with the message we're just not good enough, then we treat others badly, too. We worry about terrorism in the outer world, while harboring an attacker within. My women's group calls this voice inside "the bun lady." The war within is also outside of us. How can we change one without the other?

When I'm depressed or thoroughly disgusted with someone, my stomach hurts. If I go deep enough under the turmoil, I find an inner violence. There's a witch inside that's so fearful, enraged, blaming, self-critical, and self-destructive that it endangers my life force, deadens my creativity, and makes me want to curl up in a ball. Guilt and fatigue then can make me work too hard but never let me rest. "Go, go, go, beeee somebody," the voice says. So often when I'm not happy with myself I project it outwards, judging myself and others. This is inner hatred that results in pointing the finger outwards. Maybe I need to dig deeper and let the inner critic really have a hairball. What would life be like without this inner condemnation? Maybe I'd enjoy my garden without focusing on the weeds, find happiness in my partner even when he's forgetful. I'd slow down, feel grief, and much more joy. If my negative voice didn't make me worry, I might actually get creative or take the day off and sit over the Sunday paper, knowing the "to do" list can wait. Maybe I'd chat with my family and friends.

The critical witch is buried as deeply in humans as it is in my own consciousness. People who come to my practice are often dealing with a form of inner torture. Their anguish takes a thousand forms, but like a crown of thorns, the critic afflicts their bodies with exhaustion and despair. Perhaps worst of all, it causes separation, blame, and shame: "I can't enjoy a donut; I shouldn't be an artist; I'm too needy if I want a partner, I hate so and so, too fat, too flat." On and on it drones.

Men, too, drive themselves with work or have eating attacks or affairs to prove they're enough. If we identified the critic as our real problem, we probably wouldn't feel so enraged, condemning of each other and ourselves, or want to attack. Emptiness would be easier to bear, because we'd accept ourselves and others. We'd feel loss, but we'd be gentler with it and more open to gratitude.

Self-criticism magnifies our pain and anger, making it unbearable instead of surmountable. The unwelcome judge carries a huge concrete hairball heavy with hatred and self-loathing. The critic makes me not care, not want to bother, see no hope; it makes me run from responsibility, judge others, or watch TV, sleep, eat, or whatever.

Now I understand the old saying, "There's no rest for the wicked." I so easily sell out my dreams and wishes with this witch inside. The inner tyrant has such ideas as, "I won't be able to retire or it's okay if I don't exercise for hours. It's someone else's fault." The tricky part is that physical exercise is wonderful for my whole being, but only if I can quiet the witch and enjoy myself. The dutiful, pushy energy inside is tricking instead of treating me.

I want my voice, but every time I speak I hear an echo saying, "You shouldn't have said that." My critic says I'll look silly or stupid. If I laugh real loud, the mean old lady inside says, "Be quiet." But she's the one who needs to be silenced, not me.

This dungeon enslaves our personal power like a ball and chain, and it's the reason getting out the hairball is so important. Like a cat, we can release negativity that makes us sick, sluggish, or keeps us sitting in a corner. Watch out for fatigue or the words, "Why bother?" The witch is insidious.

Perhaps the terrorist is just afraid, lashing out at the world and at me when it feels crushed. Like Adolph Hitler, who never felt loved as a little boy, rage is rooted in early abuse. We learn to lash out.

If only little children were all heard instead of punished; maybe we'd have world peace.

## HAIRBALLS FOR THE READER

What criticisms does your inner witch make toward you? Other people?

Do you believe these accusations?

In what ways could you contribute to tranquility instead of turmoil in the world, by not listening to your critic?

# Curling Up in a Ball
## Learned Helplessness

*I have attempted to show how deeply the pattern of self-blaming and repressed anger flows, how we have a very complex set of experiences that act together to make us feel terrible about ourselves, and completely despairing of any right or power to change things.*

Michael Lerner
*Surplus Powerlessness*

What to do with anger? Listen deeply to your longings and then make requests or choices that serve you. Anger stems from a deep fear of powerlessness. It flames up from a longing for love, never met. We can continue to battle each other or harm ourselves and our environment with it. We can race to action and obsessive addiction and activity.

But, like Swiss cheese, there's always another hole. We can run or eat to the point of obesity without touching the real need. Whether we shut down, eat, barricade ourselves, or fight others, it's wasted energy and false consumption. Fat is simply unused energy. The bread we consume is like flour and water, glue gumming up our movement. We so often go towards unavailable people, draining endeavors or never-ending conflicts when we don't like ourselves.

To be happy we have to let ourselves be known, have the courage to express our convictions without attacking and just stand there. "You can't stay in a relationship," says Geneen Roth, "a healthy growing one, if you are not willing to stop focusing on what's wrong with the other person and be truthful with yourself." In *Food Is Not Love,* she says, "Breaking free from compulsive eating and participating in a mutually supportive relationship require the same thing: the willingness to stop defending yourself against pain."

In self-defense we stuff ourselves with carcinogens. Our bodies, like the earth, are dying of toxins. This is our own self-destructiveness. We hate ourselves and compete with each other. We rarely give compliments because we're so crusty from being tossed aside. We swallow feelings, become impatient, stay flabby from ambivalence, "Yes, no, yes, no."

The loving but solid inner female in all of us, the Wild Woman, the unashamed voice in men or women, can break through a half-lived life and salvage intimacy. She is the force inside that can speak up for our desires. But she's also called "the nag" because when we do ask for what we want, we're labeled too demanding or aggressive. As Sherrie Hite, author of *The Hite Report,* says, "How paradoxical that by doing this emotional work, women are making relationships possible. How ironic, then, to put women down for this."

"Get off your high horse," we tell ourselves; then we fall from our wild mare. We get clingy because we've denied our core needs, and now we want to scream them out. But it doesn't work to close down. In fact, everyone sees the ostrich with its head buried. Denial is the thing that most repels love. For example, distressed, brittle high-maintenance people are that way because they're afraid of embracing that child inside that was never treated gently. They can't say, "I'm in a lot of pain, and I'd like some help." These are people who go toward the wrong relationships or activities to make requests that will always be rebuffed.

They've hidden their grief, even to themselves, so their longing becomes exaggerated or projected, as does any feeling when we deny its existence.

We believe our needs are bad, so we disown our desires and our intellect, pain, exuberance, anxiety, sexuality, and anger rather than walk away or stay and tell our truth. We take our desires to withholding people or environments when we don't feel entitled. Go toward people and places that want you: Don't go to the desert for water!

We've learned helplessness because we're afraid of abandonment or conflict, even though this leaves us lifeless. Dana Crowley Jack says in *Silencing the Self*, "To take one's feelings seriously, to acknowledge and consider them, pulls one beyond the confines of ordinary thought. Authentic feelings can also require action by making a person too aware, too unhappy to remain within the status quo." But we hide in confusion, not even wanting to know our own truth.

When I quit a job without a backup plan, I was terrified. But I knew I was dying a slow death there. I drove to work every day with coffee and prayers. I rattled along on the freeway, waving to truck drivers, asking for good things, no longer wanting to be a victim.

I had to calm the frightened part of me every day, but instead I found a way to write this book.

In my clients I often see a great fear of being laughed at. They have a child inside who is being good, terrified of being criticized. "We are," as one client put it, "afraid of being burned again so we play it safe." The irony is that when a healthy child falls down and goes boom, it gets back up again; it doesn't sit in the corner. A healthy child dusts itself off and gets back in the ball game.

## HAIRBALLS FOR THE READER

Are there ways in which you believe you are helpless, so why try?

What have you been holding back on doing because you fear the risk? What would you be willing to do to get back in the game?

How might you need to redirect yourself so that you move towards people and places that support you with respect?

# Speaking Out

## What To Do With Anger

*When can we start resolving our differences instead of trying to drown them with time?*

Sylvia Hasvitz, Selection from
*Healing Our Planet, Healing Ourselves*

I screamed into the phone at a friend. (We have an agreement that I can do this.) I felt better, stronger, like Humpty Dumpty after all the pieces had been put back together again. I was grounded by my own anger. It wasn't the rage that did it, but hearing my own voice. I listened to myself in horror. No one told me I was wrong. No one told me I was too much, that my dreams were grandiose. No one said I was too emotional and didn't know what I was talking about. I realized after venting, when you've been wounded as a child, you take things personally. When rage floods me, I need to check out the reality. I often believe someone's taking something away from me. So, today I walked taller. I spoke up about my ideas and my vision. I was not small, crunched up, or shrunken. I was able to think clearly about my longings after getting out my hairball with a trusted friend.

Tonight I got nervous before I spoke to a group about something that I was recommending. As I got ready to speak, there was that same old voice in my head—crawly, crummy, sickening, snakelike—saying, "Weellll now, is that really what you want? Don't you think you look dumb right now? It's not going to work!"

I got through that meeting, but later found myself in a personal situation that made me want to sink down and squish my energy into a ball again. I surprised myself, however, and suddenly told my partner firmly, "I am tired of walking on eggshells, namby-pambying around. You phone and then hang up. I don't know what you want or why you keep calling me. Let's get the cards on the table. Let's either finish this relationship or decide how to go forward." With a lion's roar, I said, "I am tired of being afraid that when I say what I feel, you are going to bolt. I want to talk until we are complete." We are good friends now.

I thought I was anxious in the face of other people's anger, but that's not it. I am scared to death of my own. Sometimes I have to hold back my rage like a team of wild horses because I want to be part of solutions, not war. I stay in this tiny-tot, nice person role. It's boring, depressing and flat, like lying in a coffin. Then I project the problem onto someone else. "It's her," I say to myself. "She is so crabby and critical; I don't want to be around her." Or, "It's him." As soon as I owned my own fury, I was able to redirect it towards articulating my opinions and needs and spend an entire evening with a woman whose hostility used to make me uncomfortable. I quit projecting. I felt like one strong lion sitting calmly next to another. It wasn't that I needed to be mean or bitter; I just felt more comfortable knowing I have a roar if I choose to use it. But I can also hold back until I'm more responsible with it. I don't use it often because the world doesn't need more battles.

We could solve so many conflicts if we accepted our own dark side and allowed it in other people. We're all out of the ball field at times. But, sometimes my anger lets me know what I truly need. I don't have to dump it on people, but I can pay attention to how its passion might help me know the desires of my heart.

## HAIRBALLS FOR THE READER

How do you express your anger?

Does your style include asking for what you feel, need, and want?

Does it bother you when those you love get angry?

How could you direct your anger towards providing solutions?

# Chapter Three

## How Hairy is Dating?

## Hairy Hairball

### On Love and Fear

*So long as we are not in contact with our own personal potential, we are vulnerable to being controlled by others. If we do not know ourselves, we cannot stand to our own truth and are, therefore, in constant danger of invasion by others, male and female.*

Marion Woodman
*Addiction to Perfection*

For the past hour I've been typing furiously about sex and just lost the whole thing in my computer. Sometimes I could just cry.

But it doesn't matter because I was getting out my hairball. I was writing about my fear of being vulnerable. I never learned at home, school, or anywhere else that sex had to do with love. So I formed an unclear idea of both.

Nowadays, I realize my real problem is not sex, but learning to love. I used to act out sexually, contort myself, dating, flirting, and fantasizing—when what I really longed for was to love and be loved. I was so moved when a friend told me this week she'd cried when her partner touched her face during lovemaking. I realized that that's never happened to me. In 25 years of having intercourse, no one has ever touched my face.

I wonder when I ask my partner for things, why doesn't he give them? Is he too afraid, angry, or passive aggressive? Are we both so anxious about expressing our unmet needs that we end up feeling weird, blunted, or absent with intimacy? It's hard to feel turned on when you're sitting on a hairball. In the end, if we don't speak of our needs, pain, or fear, we feel farther apart. Sometimes admitting our fears is powerful.

My mother used to cry for my dad to bring her "just one red rose." I remember as a child nagging him. I pleaded with him to do it. I asked, "Don't you know this is her longing? She tells me about it all the time with such a faraway look. For her the rose is romantic, and she wonders why she asks but you never do it." He was silent, as always.

What was the hairball he had inside? It seems there must have been some things he wanted, too, but couldn't say. Maybe he could not assert his own needs, so holding in his hairball was a way to punish Mom. At his funeral Mom was angry. Someone had sent flowers to the graveside with no note, and she was jealous. The same issues were present in death as in life. She was enraged, because once again, the flowers weren't for her. Even in his grave, perhaps withholding was his only form of expression.

Do we withdraw or fight because of fear? It might not seem warm and cuddly to get the hairball out, but it could be good foreplay. Sex is just another form of conversation.

## HAIRBALLS FOR THE READER

Do you confuse love with sex, looking for one when you really want the other?

Are there ways you could bring more love into your sexuality or more sensuality into your life?

Does fear stop you from self expression?

What do you need to feel more sexy and loving?

# FRAZZLED OVER MY BOYFRIEND
## Anger and Confusion

*What you don't like or have rejected in yourself, you tend to project onto others...*

Harville Hendrix, Ph.D.
Helen Lakelly Hunt, Ph.D.

I get so angry and frustrated at times with this guy I'm dating. Sometimes I'm even repulsed by him. These horrible negative feelings flood me. It's so depressing. What's this about?

I want a relationship so much, but I can't seem to get the pieces to fit. I look at him: he's nice looking, bright, and fun. Yet, something inside me just doesn't click when we're together. I don't know if it's my inability to have intimacy or maybe there's just not enough chemistry. He makes me want to spin like a top.

I ask for so much advice that I want to scream from the rooftop, "What makes authors and therapists think they know what I should do in my relationship?" Sometimes other peoples' opinions are not right for us. We have to sort through it ourselves.

I've heard the absolute range of wisdom on this now. From, "He's not strong enough for you, spineless. I suffered like that myself for years." To, "This is the best thing you've ever had, don't blow it. This guy is kind and sweet, and he even wants to talk about feelings."

I think the feedback makes me more insane than the relationship! I feel so tense inside. Part of me says, "Relax; it must be you. You're too fussy." Another part says, "Get out; move on; face it, it's not the right thing."

Then another voice says, "Come on, you'll be 54 years old this year; you've dated everyone in the state. Don't you know by now what you have and how good it is?" But if it's so great, why can't I enjoy it?

Last night I read a book on abuse and neglect and decided I wanted out. Then I found a talk show about commitment, and my head spun around again like an owl. I mean, maybe it would be healthy to be with him. Are my expectations too high? Does true love always involve work?

I'm at my wits end over this, back in therapy, and on antidepressants—again. I hate being angry and critical of my partner all the time. I want to understand my reactions. Am I carrying his anger? Am I irritable like my mother?

I'm anxious all the time, afraid he'll abandon me or betray me. Am I that paranoid, overly sensitive, and never satisfied? Or is my intuition right, and he just isn't the right one for me?

I've decided after writing this I just don't have a good gut feeling about this. I called him and said, "Good-bye." Sometimes my gut is right, and I question myself too much. This diary entry has helped.

My flannel pajamas with the airplanes on them sure do feel good tonight.

## HAIRBALLS FOR THE READER

In your most intimate relationship, what triggers your anger? Why?

Does your irritability give you information about yourself?

Write until you find peace with yourself and acceptance of others.

# I Love the Laughter
## The Joys and Sorrows of Living Alone

*Love is the active concern for the life and growth of that which we love. Where this active concern is lacking, there is no love.*

Erich Fromm
*The Art of Loving*

It's really hard to laugh when you live alone. I laugh a lot more often when I'm with a partner. It's just the way it is. When I lived alone, I tried laughing. I talked to the cats a lot and smiled and grunted at email messages. Sometimes the TV even gave me a full-bellied guffaw. But mostly, it was an effort for me to laugh alone. As a single woman, I started talking to myself and I could chuckle a little bit, but I felt stupid out in the backyard, mumbling like a psychotic. I am grateful I spent years alone though, as I found out how to sit with myself.

But, people contact includes more grinning, more guffaws. Once in a while at a sports event or while shopping with friends, I found myself roaring with laughter. I must say being single was fun at times. I'm glad I did it; I enjoyed going dancing, flirting, and unraveling mysterious men.

Laughter is almost as good as sex. There's a moment of ecstasy, you merge with others, and it's satisfying for awhile.

I have dated every man in the state of California. I probably looked for Dad in the process, and I know I became addicted to male attention. I'm proud that I left no stone unturned! I learned a lot about dating and myself and laughed a lot in the process. I found out that no one is perfect. I shopped hard for the perfect man; that didn't help. I sat at home and waited for the "right" man to find me; that didn't work either. I found that dating someone who's too much like me doesn't always work, because it's more difficult to support each other when we're both strong-willed or needy. I learned (the hard way) that if a man has never been married and says he does not want a commitment, it probably means he doesn't. Most of all, I found out that people just are the way they are and trying to get them to change is useless. So, I have since embarked on being one-half of a couple.

The relationship I'm in now happened a bit backwards. My latest partner and I started out as friends. But one day he just looked so cute. His adorable dimples surfaced. His hair sparkled in the sun. I became very nervous. I noticed I had enjoyed his company for many months. I liked his values. We communicated well. Something must be wrong! Then I put him to the test without realizing what I was doing. I pushed and rebelled and argued. With a burst of venom I even criticized him and rebuked him, thinking that would be that. He's still around. We've become friends. I'm learning from dating.

The other day while watering the lawn in my bathrobe (I like to shower after I work in the garden), he stopped by and couldn't stop giggling at my big bulky red robe, slippers, and hairpins holding my frizzy hair back.

The nozzle on the hose wasn't tight enough, and I was soaked! So, now I laugh much more. I giggle like a teenager. Dating him a lot, I'm getting better at expecting less, while still holding onto my wishes. I'm learning to have men friends.

Laughter just leaps unexpectedly out of my mouth, usually when I'm being most honest. I smile much more, having pals to toss the ball back and forth with. I'm learning how to "share" with male friends.

## HAIRBALLS FOR THE READERS

Do you have more joy when with other people?

What keeps you from being closer to others?

# Dating on the Spin Cycle

## Love'em or Leave'em?

*Intimacy is, as understood here, an individual's ability to talk about who he or she really is and to say what they want and need and to be heard by the intimate partner.*

Maggie Scarf
*Intimate Partners*

Dating is like being inside a washing machine: you get turned topsy-turvy. This month, I'm seeing a guy with money who's crazy about me. I think to myself, "Self, this is a good thing; try to like this guy. He's decent, a good communicator, and helpful." But I can't get past the fact that he's short and incredibly skinny. When we hug, I can feel his bones.

Then, I get a phone call from the "X." He's got no money, doesn't keep appointments, and is a terrible communicator - but I still love him. I try to talk myself into liking dating, but it's horrible, worse than job interviews. I try to like guys I know are good for me, but it's hard. I like being excited! So, I decided I'll go for chemistry and just insist he's in therapy with me in tough times.

Is juice what we should marry for? Is friendship more important? What is love? It's this weird feeling in my gut that makes me look forward to seeing him. It's exciting to be with him. Even when we fight, we might as well be speaking different languages, but it's alive. It's complete insanity; sometimes we don't work out the kinks for months, but we're real.

And then a new guy comes into my life. He's very tall, says all the right things, brings me flowers, takes me to great places, and seems to read books. But, he kisses me constantly. On the first date, kiss, kiss, kiss. In the movie theater, his sweaty hand won't let mine go. Then he plants a real wet kiss on my neck. I'm thinking to myself, "How can I feel anything yet? This is like kissing a stranger." I can't breathe, my back tenses. I finally tell him to back off. Boy, am I learning to tell the truth! I am now able to hang out with different people, and it's good practice. How can we learn in a vacuum?

Hmm. Where's that guy I was really attracted to, who just quit calling?

## HAIRBALLS FOR THE READER

Do you know what you most want in a relationship?

What do you need to learn in order to connect better with others?

What would you like to do differently?

# Bye-Bye Baby Hairball
## On Rejection

*Stop complaining or feeling sorry for yourself about what you don't have, and instead, ask yourself what you truly want!*

Erin Brockovich
*Take It From Me*

In a relationship, I always bump into the same godforsaken issue: is it okay to be me or do I have to be someone else? There always seems to be something he wants me to be more of: mellow, busty, toned, successful but still sweet—whatever. I find myself wishing I were younger or had a flatter stomach and liked high heels. At midlife, this is getting old already. I never imagined being single at this age. I wouldn't have guessed I'd be mowing my own lawn or carrying the groceries to the car in 100-degree heat.

I met a guy six months ago, and I knew that it was a long shot. It took me a couple of weeks to return his phone call. I knew his type well: kind of cute, tall, plays a guitar—not a good start. Everybody knows guys like that are Peter Pans. They're charming, lanky, blue-eyed monsters: darling little donuts rolled in white powder. They're irresistible, but once you've had them you wish you'd gone for the brussels sprouts instead. They're cute but don't take you anywhere except on a momentary high. I'm a sucker for the darling ones because they make me feel special. For a while I imagine I'm a princess, and then the real world sets in.

I thought I was strong. I told myself I could open my heart again and take the fall if that was where it went. Before the first call, I made an agreement with myself that I wouldn't go down for the count if it didn't work out. I made a conscious decision that this was a bad bet, and I was right. He came close, but this one was just two years out of a long marriage, saying his divorce was over, but he was just not quite ready.

He dumped me. I don't know why I sort of enjoy saying it that way. Maybe it's sideways sarcasm, a defense mechanism, and a way of not admitting how hurt I feel. I think the real truth is I feel stupid.

This relationship triggered my worst fears: that I'll be abandoned and judged for being me. If my boyfriend says I'm fat or too vocal, it triggers my own inner critic. Those criticisms from my partner go right through my skin, and I'm in anguish like a dog with a bone. Growling, waving my jaw wildly from side to side, I want to throw this man to the outfield. "If you don't want me the way I am, then bye-bye, baby; so long!"

I don't know that he even thought of such criticisms, but dating always magnifies my own fears about not being enough. It's like one of those carnival houses full of strange mirrors.

Then, the old archetypal female in me sneaks in and slyly says, "If only you could wear long dresses, feed him bonbons, and always be good."

Oh geez, gimme a break! I've spent half my life learning about lipstick and skillful communications. To heck with it, I just want to be me. I struggle so to like myself the way I am and feel deserving of real relationships. Louise Hay says in *Empowering Women*, "How many times have you blamed yourself when a man is out of line?" When I really look inside at my responsibility and my part in being single, I know I'm afraid of intimacy, and rejection is hard. But, I gotta stay in the game. I'm usually analyzing all the outer things, like how many men are available in my age group or how few live in my small town. But I watch myself avoid eye contact with most people, and I notice that, when socializing, part of me always wants to flee. I feel like a jumping bean inside. I get nervous when I hang out. I pick unavailable partners unconsciously to keep space. I'm afraid to receive and surrender to love.

I find ways to avoid closeness to others. Sometimes called "emotional anorexia," this is the most deadly addiction among my neuroses. I know I withdraw from people, isolate, and get too busy to connect. I'm still a little girl who felt fragile and afraid of saying no. I still believe it's bad to have opinions, pitiful to have pain, and inappropriate to say what I feel. I fear I'm outrageously different. Yet, having my heart open is my only happiness.

Darn it! I'm me. Maybe I'm quirky, but I kind of enjoy being me, neuroses and all. Those who don't can move out of my way, cuz I'm gathering up my cowboy boots and getting ready to do some rockin'.

## HAIRBALLS FOR THE READER

Have you given yourself the opportunity to let your hair down lately? When?

Whose judgments are the most difficult for you to bear? Why?

Is there something risky or fun you're willing to do to connect with dates, partners, or people?

# How Can I Miss You When You Won't Go Away?

## Divorce and Loss

*Sometimes, the real and only victory is knowing when to walk away.*

Erin Brockovich
*Take It From Me*

I've had a couple of relationships I never got over, even though I was the one who broke them off. They haunt me like an old wound that aches whenever the barometric pressure rises. Memories of these relationships fill my body at unexpected times with unsolved mystery and longing. I believe true love doesn't heal until it's attended to; it follows us until we live it through.

The reason the body feels anguish with the very thought of a lost beloved is that divorce or separation leaves us broken. That's why the wound stays sore; it's a reminder so painful that it burns us out. We don't want to stand in the fire of a divorce or death, but we learn from the heat. There's no other way.

I've heard it's possible to take an easier route, find a more compatible partner, move on and let go, have a calmer existence, but I wonder. Maybe that's for healthier people than me. All I know is my heart hurts when something is lost or damaged that I hold dear; especially when the part that's ripped or torn seems to require care from the very person who broke it apart.

You can run; you can find another; you can go to a different town; you can become really busy. But lost love is always looming; a ghost that reappears in the scent of something familiar, in dreams and unexpected moments, even with another lover, like a haunting. The people we love are there to teach us. If we run from them, they stay in our souls.

Unfinished business, memories, and old hurts, the sensation of something from the past that lingers. Old relationships echo in us until we wrestle with them. They keep us from moving forward. We need to get the hairball out to know our truth.

Coming to peace with an ending requires a different resolution for each of us. It's possible we should never have left that person. Maybe there was something we could have learned, but we chose to bolt instead. Perhaps whatever needed to be faced was excruciating but is still necessary. Perhaps going back together is the answer and setting out to repair the relationship. Maybe there's no resolution because anger, loss, or rejection are still lodged inside. Or could it be, we're addicted to abusive people, afraid we can't do better?

It's a mystery, the persistence of longing. Sometimes we just need to stop obsessing and find someone new. Or maybe we owe it to ourselves to turn and speak to ghosts rather than take them to the grave. But how do we cough up the hairball and move on? Can we let go and complete our relationships so we feel cleansed? What helps us heal? My answer is persistence and trial and error. Clearing up stuck feelings calls for us to persevere and try different paths.

Sometimes prayer works for me; sometimes it's been a long process of talking it out. At other times giving it a break, taking time away, has done it. There were times the other person just had to cut me off, for I would hang on much too long, clinging as if to a mother like a puppy dog to milk. Cleaning up unfinished business might mean having a good argument or it could be the simple act of bringing someone a basket of fruit, but the essential ingredient in letting go seems to be courage. For me, letting go is an act of bravery and humility.

Separation is most grueling for me when I blame others. I criticize the loved one so that I won't have to struggle with my own issues. I tell myself the other person was the problem: impossible to talk to, too angry or not aware enough. But if I look deeper, I realize that war takes two.

True closure requires me to confront myself, then demands that I grieve and say what it is I wanted and what my responsibility was in creating the problems. Being accountable and taking an inventory of my part in creating the turmoil doesn't mean all of it is my fault. Obviously some relationships were easier to let go of while others were very tough. Sometimes one person loves more than another. Or the other was unhappier all along than they admitted.

Awakened at midnight, I sob, realizing the truth. I scream into the night, "I wanted you to stay, to try harder, to talk. I wanted you to be there for me and you weren't." I release my death grip, stop clutching my pillow, and utter my real feelings. "Holding on to the past is too excruciating. It stops me from moving on, from flowing forward. I must let go, forgive."

Just what is it that finally completes the circle? Am I brave enough to state my intent? Usually it means being more vulnerable than I like, getting out the deepest hairball of all. Do I have the guts to say, "I still love you. I'm sorry we feel so separate?"

In the end, speaking up seems to be the great healer, especially with a safe other. Getting the hairball out opens space, clearing the way for something new, for saying the most tender truth. Maybe it means being brave enough to reunite, surrender to commitment or accept something imperfect. Maybe it's being strong enough to say good-bye if the magic's gone and we've hung on out of fear. It might be that we need to feel our resentments or hurts towards an early childhood figure, as well as the lost love, one final time in order to be empowered to take back our own lives.

Each situation is different, but all relationships are part of the luminosity in us, the light that doesn't want to die. So, find your own way out of the jungle and then bow to the past. It is done.

## HAIRBALLS FOR THE READER

Do you have unfinished business with a past relationship?

What do you feel you need to know in order to move on?

What would you most like to say to this person to be able to find closure?

If you cannot speak it, then can you write it? Take responsibility for your part in it.

# Chapter Four

## Sex

2 A.M.

# Curve Ball Confusion

## What Makes Coupling Work?

*To love somebody is not just a strong feeling - it is a decision, it is a judgement, it is a promise.*

Eric Fromm
*The Art of Loving*

Everyone I know is pulling out whatever's left of their hair over relationships. We grew up believing in knights in shining armor, but three divorces later, many of us found it was an illusion. My girlfriend calls it "the myth of dependency."

As we age, we really spin our heads trying to figure out what we can realistically expect in our love lives. I mean talk about getting a hairball out; this intimacy stuff is a minefield. Is it possible to have love, romance, money, intellectual compatibility, and sex? The books on positive thinking say you can have it all; the Zen books tell you to give up all your desires. Each insight has a different curveball. My girlfriends wonder if they can find a more perfect man. My men friends want multiple sex partners, freedom, and someone low maintenance who does dishes and doesn't nag or yell.

Can't I find an intelligent, mature, sexy man with money who adores me? Who gave us this myth that living in two's is natural, and this thing called love is easy? I get scared to commit when I go into a new relationship, because I know the tidal wave of disappointment and hurt is just around the corner. All my baggage, my years of sensitivity to rejection, and my unmet needs await in relationship.

Is it so wrong, so narcissistic and demanding to want it all? It takes all the energy I have just to make a living, let alone deal with dating and my constant perfectionism!

How much can one get out of life? My therapist says you pick your values, then you live with the consequences.

The last guy was fun and generous. I loved his parents. But he never wanted to go hiking. If I asked, he'd say, "No way." (Not a real tactful guy.) He loves cars, I like reading. Getting him to a bookstore lecture was tough. But he was so funny that I often fell off my chair in hysterics. After awhile I just got fed up instead of fed by fun. Was I asking too much?

On our last date, he watched sports while I read existential philosophy. I finally got on the phone with a girlfriend asking, "Is this all there is?" Maybe I'm too fussy and the hard lesson is to be more patient and accept imperfections. Maybe I'm trying to fill a hole that is too infinite. I think women tend to be more like a cactus and more picky than men. Our reproductive instinct and conditioning makes us look for the right protector. But, I suspect the secret to good relationships is acceptance.

In the meantime, I still want to pursue my dreams and not squish myself into a box before I'm finally laid to rest. Learning to not blame and to communicate are keys. Being honest, asking for feedback, and learning to care for ourselves and one another is imperative. Being comfortable with who you are makes you vibant.

## HAIRBALLS FOR THE READER

What are the three main things you want in an intimate relationship?

Can you be happy with one or two of them? Why? Why not?

# Mixing and Matching Hairballs

## Understanding the Opposite Sex

*If we listen to our heart, we may feel no reservation at all about becoming involved with this person. Yet as soon as we begin to consider what kind of relationship we want, we find ourselves in the realm of conditions.*

John Welwood, Ph.D.
*Journey of the Heart*

Dating is weird. Maybe arranged marriages make more sense—nice and tidy, managed by someone else, time to do other things. Who knows? I got so sick of it, I decided not caring was the trick, being self-sufficient.

So, I go to a political meeting thinking, "This is good; I am being intelligent, I am independent. If I meet a man here, that's OK. I'm doing my own thing." Of course, I meet a man. He's dynamic, informed, funny: a real match. We go out after the meeting. The conversation is fascinating. I say to my self, "Self . . . get real. Find out what this guy's agenda is. You need to be practical." These are my thoughts as we are carrying on a conversation about politics.

Then I get my nerve up. It's time for the hairball to come out, so I say, "Listen, I need to ask you something. Are you single or what's your status?" He says, "I'm married and intend to stay that way. I'm unhappy and don't have sex anymore, but I'd never leave my family. I do have affairs and have been attracted to you."

I want to say, "What kind of a life is that? Can't you even talk to your wife? Are you really going to live like this? What kind of courage is that?" But he seems like a good career contact, so I keep my hairball down with the help of guacamole and lots of taco chips.

I wonder, "Is this an epidemic? This is the fifth man I've met this month who is telling me the same thing. Is it something I'm putting out?" I tell him tactfully that I hope we can be colleagues in business. Dating requires a Sherlock Holmes. It's really insane. The recently divorced ones are illusive, the married ones are seductive, the guys on web dating seem to want tall blondes.

I get home. The guy I met the week before said he thought I was the greatest, but he never called back. The old boyfriend I'm trying to let go of, who is afraid of commitment, of course called me.

This is dating? I guess you have to be willing to kiss a lot of frogs and keep your bifocal eyeglasses on.

## HAIRBALLS FOR THE READER

Do you ever attract relationships that aren't good for you?

What messages might you be putting out there to attract such men (or women)?

What stops you from going for what you want? Describe it.

# On Living Alone

## Self Love

*Like self--starvation with food or compulsive dieting or hoarding with money, deprivation with sex can make one feel powerful and defended against all hurts.*

Patrick Carnes

*The Betrayal Bond*

Today I woke up with thoughts crawling all over my body like black spiders from my inner critic, "the witch," saying, "Boy, are you tired. You are getting older. My God, look at you in that mirror! Ach!" Then I go out with friends. They keep saying, "Your hair is different, it's white," then long pause— "Oh, I like it." Sure.

"Get a cup of coffee," I mumble, stumbling around in my faded bathrobe. Then I sigh, "I am so glad I've been single. If I had been in a relationship sooner, what would he think of these puffy eyes?"

Dating reminded me of shopping at Macy's: I kinda knew what I wanted, but couldn't find it and then I'd get so tired of shopping that I ended up going home with nothing. Or, if I get something, I end up returning it. It just doesn't quite fit.

Talking with one of my friends yesterday, I realized this isn't even about the man. I have to learn to live with myself. Looking back, I see now why I have been single so long. I needed to see what it was like living with me.

Why weren't my relationships working? Because living with me wasn't easy. As long as a man was around, I could never tell if it was him or me that was the problem. Living alone, I realized there are my moods; there are my depressions; there are my disappointments; my difficulty with discipline, decisions, and health. There's no one else to blame.

If I could learn to live with me, then I could let others be themselves and it won't ruin my day. As Louise Hay says, "Today, an unmarried woman has the whole world in front of her. She can rise as high as her capabilities and her belief in herself." I don't have to let moody or hostile people knock me off course. It's my own fear I have to grapple with. I stay in touch with myself by writing in my journal and spitting out my own hairball.

So, I went to an art festival by myself today and just watched all the married couples as I sat on a big rock. They all had pot bellies and wore funny looking worn shoes, thongs flapping along. I thought to myself, "I'm having fun here today, meeting people and chatting. I like myself! And it surely seems to me that the happiest couples are ordinary folks, not trying so hard to be perfect."

Living alone gave me time for cleaning up my life. I have learned that love is not made up of a wish list of characteristics, like ordering from a catalogue. It comes sooner when we like ourselves or when we drop the walls we've constructed around ourselves. Do some people find the perfect mate when they have high self-esteem? Or when they're comfortable living alone? Maybe. But I think most of us just have to keep our hearts open, watch the bouncing ball, and embrace imperfect reality.

## HAIRBALLS FOR THE READER

How do you feel when you are single? Do you like it? Why? Why not?

Have you ever blamed a partner for something that you do, too?

Are you too judgmental of others?

# HAVING A BALL HAIRBALL
## How Important is Sex?

*You usually want intimacy before you'll have sex, and he usually wants intimacy through having sex."*
Martin G. Friedman
*Straight Talk for Men About Marriage*

Why is it that half the population (including me) has stopped having sex? What's up - or not up - with that? It seems that everyone I talk to is either divorcing, single, struggling with kids at home, menopause, resentments—whatever causes lack of sex. What's up? Am I so afraid of another broken heart that I can't take a chance and enjoy my own sexuality? I mean feeling sexual is life enhancing, but it's been nothing but a dull thud lately.

Maybe I bought into some commercial idea that this would be a natural part of fulfillment in my life.

So, when do I expect to enjoy sex again, when I'm 70? What am I waiting for? What would I need in order to let sex back into my life: a commitment, marriage, finding "the one"? But, then there's possible illness, dysfunctions, or sometimes lack of desire.

I don't get it. My sexuality is important, yet I've cut it off for years. Maybe it's because I don't want to look like a whore, but the honest fact is I'm afraid to fall in love again, which unfortunately for me, I do all too easily. Sex and love always arrive hand in hand with me. So, how long do I wait? I'm really angry at the prospect of life without love and sex.

Maybe I'm just not good at being intimate. But, I'm trying to be more present with people these days, to keep the ball bouncing back and forth longer. I'm rarely the one who stops the game now. I'm out where I'm eye to eye with more people in daily encounters, and I believe that is where "intercourse" really begins - by connecting with others.

I know what I learned in church. I'm afraid that if I enjoy sex, men tend to put me in the slut department. And if I'm unavailable, that doesn't work either.

Not to mention the fear of disease! Now, I've exhausted myself again, just thinking about it all. This hairball seems to lead me to wanting to numb out. I mean; what to do? Sleep with your neighbor and use tons of condoms? Wait forever for the right person? Curl up with someone you're not turned on to and wake up with a fake smile, like, "Okay, you can leave now. I have things to do."

I'm just getting too old for this. Thank God I have my friends and my diary! It helps me sort through this. Give me one good man and years of involvement. Is that too much to ask? What happened to me months ago that put my sensuality to sleep? I took myself out of the game, started watching TV and munching popcorn.

What's stopping me from feeling my sensuality? I know once I put out the scent, it'll be a lot of work. Men I don't like will hit the ball to me and I'll have to say, "No thanks." I hate that. And so often they are the persistent ones. I've been telling one guy "No" for eight years. I even said, putting my nose right up to his, a loud "no!" Adding, "no offense, I'm not attracted to you. There's no chemistry. Stop making me squirm." He gave me a squishy kiss. He still doesn't get it! Is this pure narcissism? A couple of them phone me every week. Even when I told one, "I'm just not at *all* interested," he still kept calling!

There are men I would consider going "there" with, but I'm afraid they'd dump me afterward. So I flatten my fluffy hair or pin the hair into a tail and just do my taxes. I say, "I'll be responsible instead. I'll live a healthy, mature life, I'm self sufficient." So, when do I hold onto the ball or when do I play ball? I guess all I can do is keep being honest with myself.

## HAIRBALLS FOR THE READER

Are you expressing your sexuality to your satisfaction? Why or why not?

Is there one thing you can do to include more sensuality in your life?

# Hairballs of Fire

## The Marriage Factor

*It is easier to go without love than to accept a form of love that reawakens our fears of loss. In fact, to receive love feels far more dangerous than to be without it.*

Harville Hendrix, Ph.D.
and Helen Lakelly Hunt, Ph.D.
*Receiving Love*

I was just married and I thought I'd be in bliss. Like Cinderella reunited with her prince, I expected everything to change suddenly, like magic. I was so glad to no longer be in the "dating game."

Somehow I've always thought love was easy. Somewhere inside I still bought the idea that love is grand. Aren't I a little old to still be having my illusions shattered?

Instead of feeling peace since marrying, all the fears of my life have flooded me. I get so angry about his habits and emotionally raw from little things he does that, even I can see, are tiny, but still make me doubt I should trust him.

It's just so scary to talk to my husband about what I really feel. But, it seems that an alive marriage requires complete courage. There's no way to keep love alive without putting my feet in the fire.

I want this relationship to work. I want to be happy, but I'm so sensitive that I get overwhelmed with feelings I can't express. So, I'm crabby a lot.

I end up feeling paranoid, abandoned—feeling nuts or wanting to flee. I'm afraid if I enter into conflict, I'll never get out. I feel defeated before I start. I can't even run; I just find myself crying in a puddle.

I don't want to manage my emotions the way I have in the past, distracting myself in a million ways and paying for it in lost intimacy. I've always kept myself really busy, until close relationships lit the match again and—bingo—there were my old fears, blazing away!

I'm a master at avoiding what hurts and, sadly, at keeping myself from the one I love. I'm still too busy with my "to do" list, using substances (as much as my midlife body can handle), worrying about retirement, and doing retail therapy (shopping for those of you who don't do it!)

I can't believe I'm here again with the intimacy I want in front of me and too scared to walk through the door. I doubt facing conflict will ever be easy for me, even though I know the love we feel only surfaces when my partner and I get vulnerable and talk, sharing our deepest truths.

It seems to help when we acknowledge that inside we're still small children and that our weirdest behaviors are attempts to stay safe and avoid abuse. Our pattern is something like this: he shuts down; I get mad. He gets passive aggressive, telling me he'll do something I want, then not doing it. I make requests and want to be treated like the queen I've always wanted to be, feeling hopeful and fearful at the same time about asking for what I want. I get critical and then he says he feels inadequate. He withdraws or does something unkind because he is unable to be direct.

Once we speak these truths, we feel better. When we feel wounded, it's usually that the other person is opening old wounds. It's painful for me to realize that in this, my third marriage, I still cope with self-hatred. It's such a blow to have it still in me. If I loved myself more, his forgetfulness wouldn't trigger trauma.

Being close to another person brings these insecurities out. Perhaps this is the gift of relationships: the chance to see ourselves as we really are and find a way to accept ourselves.

Harville Hendrix inspires me. In *Keeping the Love You Find,* he says, "Marriage itself is in essence therapy."

This reminder makes me ask myself if I've run from the connections with people I've started over the years because I still haven't accomplished loving myself? How often do we flee our own flaws?

The other night I asked him, "Why don't you compliment me anymore?" I was nervous and just plain disgusted. He looked at me, just staring, then dropped his head. "Oh my God," I thought, "my hips are as wide as a bus!" Then he said, "I mean to, but I never learned it." Well, the next day it occurred to me, I feel insecure lately, especially when he's so silent; my distorted thoughts of my body were back.

I get grumpy and assume he's rejecting me. Hendrix explains what you don't like or have rejected in yourself, you tend to project onto others.

So, I got up my nerve and asked him, "Do you think my hips are too big?" He said, "I love your curves." So then I decided to get some "attitude" and I said, "Yeah, you're so skinny. Two bony people in bed just wouldn't work!" And, I strutted my stuff, walking away.

This isn't exactly the kind of heat I was looking for in love, but, reluctantly, I'm standing in the fire. Relationships require each person involved to listen carefully and speak clearly, but this is an evolution. It's a life's work. He's no prince and I'm no princess, but we do love each other, and we do have passion: hairballs of fire.

But excitement wasn't enough. We broke up. We learned in couples therapy that he had no intention on building a relationship, but rather on building his work and other activities. His work and other endeavors were more important than the marriage.

My part in it? I didn't believe I deserved a reliable partner who cared about me. Deprivation, both with food and men was an old habit. I was too desperate for love and did not regulate my reactivity well.

## HAIRBALLS FOR THE READER

Are there things about yourself that you project onto your partner?

Can you step back from your relationship in order to see what reactions are yours and which are theirs?

What is your deepest intent in the relationship?

Can you speak of your fears and wishes and offer support instead of anger?

# Chapter Five

## Workin' For a Livin'

# Back in the Game
## On Enjoying Work

*When you start doing the work you were born to do, you don't feel passion. What you feel is that nothing is missing.*

Barbara Sher
*Live the Life You Love*

This career thing is so difficult—rushing off to work in the morning with a hairball stuck in my throat. I want to poke my head out the car window and scream, "Am I making any difference in this world? I'm still working, and I wanted to be retired by now!"

This money-making thing is numbing. I'm so fearful that I can't even think about what might really turn me on. I'm dropping the ball instead of getting out the hairball.

I repeatedly end up doing things I'm not good at. I love group facilitation, public relations, talking on the phone, being involved in politics. I'm an extrovert. So what do I choose to do instead? Paperwork, writing, and struggling with cell phones and computers. I've done everything from waitressing to radio host. I finally found employment at a place I liked with a respectful employer, but the people at the top kept changing the rules. Every day something new happened without my input. One afternoon twelve people were fired and my workload doubled. My colleagues used to laugh about how my hair stood on end, stuck out the side of my head. I felt so disempowered, I quit.

My flow gets blocked when I feel like I'm a part of a machine and I don't do what I do best. I tighten up so much and get so busy, so frenzied trying to keep the ball rolling, that I don't stop to let out my hairball. I say to myself, "Wait a minute, stop, do something you love!" But then I get scared and confused, not knowing whether to move to Bali, buy an RV trailer, write a book, or get a job in yet another nonprofit trying to change the world.

Is it possible to love your career? Find your bliss? Why do I stay in jobs that don't fit me? Why do I keep a ball of frustration stuck in my throat instead of getting it out and moving ahead toward work I enjoy? I guess it's hard to be creative when you're buried under a mound of duties and obligations. Sometimes I don't even feel like I'm in the ball game; afraid to make a change, I stay in the bleachers. Of course every job includes doing things you don't like to do, but do you ever feel like you're just in the wrong place?

I trust that if I continue to talk and write about my real needs, doors will open so I can leave the job that doesn't work and into one that suits me. For everyone, there is a different solution—downsize and be an artist, stick it out and get retirement, start your own business, whatever. I'm scared to leap from this work into nothing, but I've tried too long to figure out a backup plan. I'd rather have faith that I'll find my way. They told me today to lay off more people. Then one of my favorite managers relocated. I quit!

## HAIRBALLS FOR THE READER

What is one small step you can take towards doing what interests you?

What do you do best?

When are you the happiest?

# Driving the Ball

## Accomplishing Goals

*The secret to removing the harmful effects of feeling stressed and under pressure is to be in the now...I choose to feel good while I'm in the moment, attracting into my life the manifestations of my desires.*

Wayne Dyer
*The Power of Intention*

Instead of leading meaningful, goal-directed lives, we tend to muck around in the hairball on the rug, focusing on the small details of life, never on what we really want. We can be overcontrolling or prickly or lie limply on the floor feeling victimized because we never learned to use our voice. We never felt deep in our bones that we could get clear on what we want and then practice directing the ball toward that.

The great leaders in history had vision. In spite of sand traps, their balls landed where they aimed them because they stated their dreams and wishes.

Some of us focus on the ball that's been lost in the rough so we can stay out of the game, or play but not win. This tendency to stare at the sandpit isn't empowering. I can so easily spiral into despair, a hopeless, tired place at the bottom of the earth. My body feels weighted down by my grandma's self-hatred, my mother's self-doubt, my father's fear, and a millennium of beliefs that are wrong and even a little loony.

I learned early to focus on dustballs and vacuuming instead of my dreams. Grandma Alice was known for being flustered and angry. She hated being called too opinionated and vocal, so she became mean instead. They say she married two charismatic, cruel husbands, both bootleggers.

All the women in her family, including me, suffer from a kind of self-doubt that takes the form of physical quicksand that floods the body, dragging it down. This feeling of not wanting to try new things or make steps toward my goals appears as a sudden complete lack of energy. I've learned that I do this when I'm beating myself up, an old habit. I get in a blur and unable to make decisions, convinced that nothing I do will be right. Out of habit, I focus on tasks that are the least fulfilling or fun.

Why do I stay in this hairball, ruminating on worries instead of on my goals and wants? I'm plagued by voices in my head saying, "I'm too old, too fat, I don't know enough, I've failed so many times, why bother?" Why are so many of us so mousy, poking and pulling on the hairball, but never making anything of it?

I tend to do everything except what really matters to me—mow the lawn instead of write, shop instead of figure out how to make more money, try to get something from the most rejecting source. The things of my heart get lost in the shuffle of life.

Self-criticism seems like a plot by the patriarchs of the world so that women never take the bindings off our feet, and men tend to suffer with defeat, staying in jobs they despise. Under the hairball of frustration in my gut is a chamber holding centuries of buried put downs, unspoken negative beliefs, and self-undoing. Deep within most women's bellies and inside men's backbones lies muffled screams that, if let out, might change the world.

Even when we think we've gotten a break from the self-talk that tears us down inch by inch, even when we've gone to the club, lost weight, or gotten married, the inner judge still attacks.

Well here's an idea: Instead of ignoring it, stuffing it, or keeping so busy it can't get to you, when you have an unpleasant emotion, think, "What choices do I have right now?" Or ask yourself, "How would I most like to handle this situation?"

It's time we come to the table with a vision of what we yearn for, or we won't be able to direct the ball to its highest destination. Start to declare your desires. Don't step on the hairball; get it to the goal line!

## HAIRBALLS FOR THE READER

Write down your overall long-term vision for what you want.

What are some short-term ways you can drive that ball forward?

As you set goals, what self-talk do you hear? Is there something you want to say in response?

# Being Nobody Special

## Clarifying Career Goals

*Most people really don't need advice. They just need support and discipline in doing what they already know works.*

Marianne Williamson
*A Return to Love*

I go to a career counselor and get my hairball out. I tell him, "I need to find out who I am. I'm fifty-six years old; why don't I know what I want to be when I grow up?"

The counselor says, "I have a feeling that you're stuck in your childhood."

I think, "This is worth eighty-five dollars?" I say, "Excuse me, are you telling me I drove two hours to hear this? I want some answers!"

He says I've been trying to prove something to my mother. He encourages me to feel that I'm enough and that maybe I need to learn to relax. I'm frustrated, my feelings are stuck in my throat, but then the hairball comes out. "Listen," I say, "I'm not going to come here for the next two years to hear this. This hairball has to move."

He says, "To get a clue, go home and write about the things you've done that exhaust you, then about the things that nourish you. When you become authentic, you'll do things that give you energy." That's great, but what about money? What if my "real" self just plays ball?

All I've realized out of career counseling is that I don't want to prove anything anymore. Maybe the career counseling will get me no career at all. Some days I think maybe I'll become a postal worker or work at a fruit stand. I no longer feel the need to be a hero.

I know that what my counselor's saying must be right: nobody's a nobody. We're all somebody. I'm just like everybody else, and in fact, I don't have it so bad. At least, where I work I'm appreciated and able to offer a service. That's gotta be good enough.

I'm cozy here at home tonight, just hanging out with my cat. I guess these sessions do relax me. I'm getting a different kind of movement out of this counseling than I'd expected. What if we all buy into a commercial idea that we have to succeed to be seen and loved? Why don't we start more communities that value hanging out?

My cat's tail is hanging over the computer screen, blocking my view, but I don't care that I can't see it clearly. I don't feel pushed, there's no time pressure. Tonight nobody is tense or congested.

Being a nobody isn't bad.

## HAIRBALLS FOR THE READER

Are you afraid you're nobody if you don't excel, stand out, receive praise? Why?

What do you appreciate about just being you?

How might you relax and accept who you are?

"I Hate Job Hunting"

# The Job of Job Hunting

## Telling the Truth at Work

*At its core, dialogue is a communication process, and it is a relationship builder. It is an 'opening process' for work groups and organizations.*

Doug Ross, Ph.D.
*A Tao of Dialogue*

How many people love their work? Even though I have a job, I still look through the want ads. Some careers sound so fascinating. There are newspapers that need reporters, storage rooms that are looking for managers, bed and breakfasts that want live-ins, foreign countries that need English teachers, political groups that need more voices: lots of adventures. I love seeing new opportunities. It's like going to Italy or China. Hey, look at this completely new workplace. Check it out.

Some people do love their work. Today I talked to a co-worker who just loves her job. I've rarely felt satisfied. Why? I can't stand the lack of honesty. I look for aliveness and rarely see it.

I always thought I should write a column reviewing job environments the way restaurants are reviewed in the "food" section. It's amazing to me how jobs vary. In some, you feel like you have to tiptoe around, as though you were in a library. In others, you find employees wearing jeans and swearing a lot. Sometimes everyone is in a hurry, and you get swept up in the current. Some places are dry and stale, and you'd better not say the wrong thing. You might find that nobody gives a damn about their job, or the turnover is so high that nobody knows what they are doing.

No matter where you work, you hardly ever find hairballs in the workplace. People rarely tell the truth or express what they feel—it's too scary. Nobody wants to get fired or risk being an outcast. It's ironic. Even though the starch is stiff in the collars, the back is upright, and words are carefully chosen, the things *not* said end up surfacing anyway: employees quit, withdraw, goof off, get laid off, are chronically late, eat sugar all day, take lots of cigarette breaks or sick days, etc. Sometimes I even convince myself I'm ill, just because I need a day off of work. Isn't it time that communication and appreciation in the workplace becomes a priority?

If we could just get our hairballs out—at least say what we feel or need—we might share a vision for our company. We might work as a team! The world would be full of people happy at their job, doing what they like, feeling appreciated.

I may have to leave another job. Why is my co-worker so content? She expects less of life. She accepts imperfections. She doesn't have a hairball. I can't keep it in any longer: this hairball is beginning to feel like a bowling ball.

## HAIRBALLS FOR THE READER

Do you have difficulty expressing your whole self to your co-workers; to your boss?

What's missing that you'd like to include while you're at work?

How could you accept imperfection in the workplace?

# Dollars and Sense

## Overcoming Money Fears

*There is a tremendous pull toward getting scared, retreating back into ways about one's self and others that feel 'more comfortable,' ways of being . . . that embody our deep fears about our own inadequacies and inevitable isolation.*

Michael Lerner
*Surplus Powerlessness*

How do I deal with money issues and move forward? I'm flooded with fear. I know I'm supposed to do affirmations or create a retirement plan, but it bores me. Am I immature? Nobody talked about money growing up. In the back of my mind, I'm always afraid I'm going to lose money or get old without having enough. I feel like I'm moving toward an unknown destiny of loneliness and death as I watch limitations set in and my body begin to sag. Growing older, I'm trying to still my fears as they magnify.

"How's my IRA? Look at the cost of these vitamins! Do I really have to do work I don't like, just for the money?" The bills come and my soul cries, "Car insurance, taxes are due, the roof leaks, and the front porch light needs rewiring."

Will I die with a credit card debt yea high? Dealing with funds seems so important, but I'd rather be out gardening or with a friend than doing math. I've had it up to here with paperwork, computers, and machines. I don't want to save, diversify, allocate, relocate, replenish, or think about dollars for retirement and my funeral!

It gets worse! I go out with my partner, and I'm feeling good. The bill arrives and I think to myself, "Self! You're liberated, you have a job, why don't you pay your own way?"

Then he says he wants me to pay for our dinner, and I'm filled with weird feelings. I think, "Why is he asking me to pay? He's the guy."

I didn't know I'd be so bothered by this. I guess I secretly like being taken care of, even though I act like I don't need to be. Is this a "girl thing"? I still carry some sort of sovereignty, like he's supposed to treat me. I feel capable of paying my own way, but am I really still dependent or spoiled? Why is it so hard to tell the truth about this?

I look at him across the table and think, "Oh God, now we have to deal with another issue. I don't know what made me think coupling would be so easy. Why's he's staring at me like I'm in a fish bowl?" What is he thinking?

Interestingly, many of the rich men I've dated have acted the most impatient or selfish in relationship. So I tell myself, "Okay, this is good. I'm liberated. I can take care of my own life. I can handle money."

But then this other voice creeps in. "You loved it when you dated rich men, and they paid for everything."

I swat at my thought like a fly. "Oh my addictive personality just loved the adrenaline rush of it all." Looking back at the fancy restaurants and flowers, the truth is it always ended in disaster for me. Maybe those meals did cost me something after all? How do guys feel about this? Was I indoctrinated as a girl? Perhaps growing as a woman means leaving the princess behind? Or, at least sharing the load, whatever that may be.

People get so cranky around money, you'd think it was a bad thing. We deal with it everyday, yet go on a date or go through a divorce or discuss it with our boss, and suddenly it's like being burned at the stake. Why don't people talk about money? Our blood pressure's rising, and everybody tries to act like it's no big deal.

It's really crazy because today women are considered to be self-sufficient, yet buried in their psyches are little Cinderellas. These two sides fight each other, and the only answer must be to try to be honest and own both.

Today I was negotiating a contract on my rental unit, and everybody was so friendly and talkative until we got to the subject of money. You would have thought someone dropped a hand grenade in the room. I guess it scares everyone and means putting up a shield.

Money is like sex. I'm either longing for it, pretending it doesn't exist, imagining there's a lot of it, taking pleasure in it, feeling too tired to deal with it, worrying about losing it, wanting tons more of it, wishing to quit everything else in my life and just devote myself to it, or wondering what happened to it?

I wish my fears about having enough money, planning for it, and trying not to lose it didn't have to underlie all my days. It's not fun, romantic, or artistic, nor is math my strong subject.

Talking to my accountant today, she says everyone is freaked about money, even rich people. It made me feel better to get it out and realize it's pretty common. She said lots of people come to the tax office fighting like cats and dogs (not that they fight much at all, the way people do!) or still carrying a paper bag full of cash receipts. She says she has to be a counselor as much as an accountant because they come in fussing so much. What's up with that?

Love and money—I feel at this late stage in life that I've known nothing about either one. But, I'm finally learning to talk about it. I guess being a grown-up means taking care of yourself. Or is surrender and service the better path?

I'd prefer the life of my cat Einstein. He doesn't worry. He's got faith, so he relaxes. He just sits on top of my computer, wondering what's all the fuss?

## HAIRBALLS FOR THE READER

Do you have enough money?

What could you do to feel comfortable with your money situation?

What aren't you doing to become independent?

# Spit It Out

## Speaking Up At Work

*The vocabulary of women who suffer from eating disorders is filled with words like shrunken, impoverished, exhausted, drained, depleted, all used up, stripped, sucked dry, totally empty, all spread out.*

Kim Chernin
*The Hungry Self*

There is great power in the spoken word. Speaking or writing our truth moves us out of inertia and fatigue. Giving voice to our desires moves energy and burns fat. We need to learn to distinguish between the voices within—to identify the internal critic and to listen to our true inner voice, which says, "Yes, go for it" or "My gut says no" or "Let go." We should be wary of therapists and advice-givers who may not support our strengths.

There are lessons to be learned in being audacious. We hold back, afraid that exhilaration or new ideas will drive people or employers away. How does one take risks? Everyone craves vitality and permission to be freely, unashamedly themselves.

I spoke up at work today, and my boss's neck turned red. She told me later she was angry. I didn't tell her what I wanted to suggest. I left her thinking that I meant something offensive, but that is not what I intended. It is so anxiety provoking to speak up that sometimes I freeze. Then I drove home in a blur, spaced out and ready for sleep much too early.

We must love and admit all parts of who we are, at work and at home—angry, timid, frightened. But it takes an agreement to talk so openly and courage to get out of that mummy pose. Though honesty makes for more aliveness and productivity, even better sex, we are afraid. As Maggie Scharf says in *Intimate Partners,* "Positive changes cannot be negotiated when neither partner has been capable of stating his own position clearly or for that matter, discovering what the other person's position might be."

It's like playing with a fastball sometimes, trying to say effectively what you feel and need. It's also an art to *not* get what you want and respect that. But, I am no longer dry from deserting myself: I'm wet. I like speaking in boardrooms and at parties and not worrying about what people think. I don't engage constantly mean-spirited people unless it's essential. I am no longer the dethroned queen. I laugh heartily, eat pizza, and talk politics. I grieve and get scared, dance and boast. I call this "pushing it through," like a woman giving birth. Speaking up at work requires of me my full self expression.

We need to put passion where neediness used to be. Wild women provide; they stoke the fire. They aren't sluggish, and good men support their exuberance. Desires of one's heart don't gather dust. When one gets true power, one doesn't have longing or resentment. In *Women Who Run With Wolves,* Clarissa Pinkola Estes says, "Mother of God! So many women themselves are afraid of women's power. If men are going to ever learn to stand it, then without a doubt women have to learn to stand it." An alive career encourages open negotiation. Evaluations are insulting, while dialogue is creative.

To my surprise, I found that my fiery side did not repel men. On the contrary, they were like moths to the flame. At work or in dating, they're attracted to this lightning, this spark. This is not the attacking, dark side of power. This is conversation that clears the air and then builds a collective vision.

As feelings began to erupt and flow and come out of my mouth like a hairball, my fat turned into energy and I came alive. I tapped into the unashamed me. My weight began to drop away, both psychic heaviness and in body. I began to give voice to my desires. Work is only work when we stop being ourselves.

## HAIRBALLS FOR THE READER

In what situation do you most often give away your power?

When do you make requests in situations that have nothing to give you?

What is one thing you can do to change that?

# Calm as a Cat
## Staying Centered

*We should go home to ourselves and practice mindful breathing and mindful walking to allow ourselves to calm down and to allow lucidity to come, so that we can understand the real roots of our suffering and the suffering of the world.*

Thich Nhat Hanh

My cat Einstein wonders why so much of my life seems like a struggle. If he could write in a diary, here's what I bet he'd say.

"Living with this woman gets more bizarre every year. I lie around and watch her go from the car to the computer, back to the fridge, to the washing machine and around in circles. Then she answers the phone: talking, talking, talking.

"Ten minutes later, her little portable phone rings and she sticks it in her other ear. Two phones, two ears – it's too much! What could she be talking about that is so important? Why doesn't she rub my belly anymore? I have to admit, though, it's kind of entertaining to watch her, especially in the morning when her big hair is flying all over the place.

"She hasn't given me enough treats lately. I wait around the coffeepot, trying to get her attention; but noooooo, she's so busy, she hardly even notices me anymore. So, I sit on top of the computer and let my tail hang down over the screen. As long as I keep wagging, she has to grab it and swing it back and forth all day long. I like it. I get petted, she gets to play, and it lightens her mood.

"I don't know why, but I don't seem to get hairballs anymore. Now she has them instead. I relax, but she gets all balled up: she's moody, has way too much to do, and scratches her head a lot. It's so warm up on this machine. I love it up here.

"She seems kind of full right now, like she's hanging on to something. I wish she'd let go of worry and cut down on the constant activity. If she would only learn from me.

"I'm calm as a cat."

This world promotes commercialism, fast pace, youth, beauty, getting ahead, and competition. Being a workaholic and having an inner critic keeps me running. How ironic that I've rested more since I sprained my ankle. I was kicked playing on a women's soccer team. Go figure! Always competing or going somewhere. I'm happy today sitting here with Einstein. What made me run to the field in my soccer shoes when I was already tired? Am I still looking for love and attention? Driven to success? For who? For what?

I always wanted to be seen and loved more as a kid. It wasn't that my parents didn't love me, but Mom was ambitious, Dad aloof, like men were supposed to be. I think my cat understands serenity better than I do.

## HAIRBALLS FOR THE READER

What helps you relax?

What stops you from calming down?

Can you honor animals this week with donations or volunteerism?

# Chapter Six

## Who Am I Really?

# Going to the Ball
## But Are We Having a Ball?

*The emotional stress of being fat in the United States is not unlike that experienced by soldiers who spend long periods in a combat zone.*

W. Charisse Goodman
*The Invisible Woman*

When I face getting dressed in the morning, I can't understand how I can have so many clothes yet wear so few. It reminds me of jobs and men: they look good, they appear attractive, but sometimes I'm just not comfortable. So many of them just aren't quite right for me. Like today, I shopped for hours and ended up disgusted, frustrated and empty.

I couldn't find my identity as I tried to fit into boots with square toes, jeans with flair bottoms, and tight pastel T-shirts.

I was determined to get a great top to go with the jeans; so what happens? I go into the teenagers' section; I love all that sexy, slinky stuff. It doesn't fit me, so I go upstairs to the grown-ups' department. Nah, it's too conservative—nice, but not sexy. I decide it must be me: I need to lose ten pounds. Now I really want to buy almost anything. There has to be something that'll cheer me up, something smart and slimming in black. I try on twenty black outfits from the sale rack—before I start to sink.

I'm in the dressing room, and I have to sit down. I end up telling the other women how good they look in their formal wear and business suits. We have a few laughs since they all think they're too fat. Everybody's tired. Children are getting lost crawling under stalls while their mothers look at price tags on prom dresses. The men wait outside, staring at the teenagers. What's it all about?

Why is this seemingly superficial topic important to me? There's something about getting dressed that seems to reflect the struggles in my life. Like today I exhausted myself and finally bought something that I probably won't wear. Why? I wanted to feel great, heighten my self-esteem. I didn't want to come home empty handed.

And hey, while I'm on a roll—what about shoes? When they look good, you can't walk in them; if you want to look sexy, you simply can't go anywhere. If you do, you're in pain or incapacitating your arches for life. Are we letting shoe manufacturers plot to keep women from standing on their own feet because they don't want us to be grounded?

Think about thongs, how they scrunch our feet and flop along. Is that real walking? Even my doctor said most women are getting bone spurs from their shoes. Why haven't we collectively screamed "no more"? I guess being cute still wins.

I want to be paid big bucks and feel sexy, but I also want to relax and walk. I guess that's many women's conflict. I feel put together and smooth when I wear suit jackets, but then I don't feel like hanging out. My baggy jeans feel the best, but I look like a sixties hippie. My butt looks big in them and no buts about it, they're certainly not seductive. I like long dresses, but they're almost too feminine, too Pollyanna for me.

Shopping is like my life: Do I bounce from rebelling to caring too much what others think? I often wear pearls and a black suit to work, but is that really who I am? Do I have to look like that to get a high-paying job, a man? Maybe the real truth, under all the costumes and masks, is that I'm scared that who I am may not be acceptable; that deep down I don't believe I'm enough.

Okay, I'm getting a breakthrough writing this. My favorite boots are red and the T-shirts are low cut. I love big glittery earrings and loud bangle bracelets. It's all about being comfortable with myself. Full expression is fun!

Watch out world, here I come!

And what's with this princess thing, with play dress up? I love jeans and rhinestones; don't know whether I want to toss a tennis ball around or go to the ball.

Sometimes I want to cut off all my hair or let it grow mousey grey and say, "What you see is what you get," but I stop because I know men like a lot of colored hair.

Even though I believe the way I dress says something about me, I'm still too much of a people pleaser, buying things other people like on me and never wearing them. They hang in the closet for years.

Sometimes I like the company of a girlfriend when I'm shopping, but then the danger is that she loves me in the zebra skirt with the bronze top, which I hate, but she insists "it's me." Two hundred dollars later, it still hangs in my closet. So, what's going on? Why do I feel like Cinderella, never making it to the ball?

This week at the thrift store my girlfriend picked out this overstuffed parka for me. It was twice my size, down to my knees, puffy, full of fluff. I felt like I was about to launch the space shuttle in it. I told her, "Jeeze, it's not really my style." Yet, just for the heck of it, I bought it. Well, I'll be darned; I wear it all the time. I feel like I'm entering a cloud when I wear it. It's warm and silky. It's solid green; I just feel natural in it.

So, what's with that? Someone knows me better than I do? I walk around wondering how I ended up with this coat that I never would have picked out. I guess we really do need feedback. We do need each other. Is the idea that we find our own way in life all wrong? Is it really too difficult to try something different, new, outside old patterns? Left to my own devices, I would have said, "It's not me." I'm cozy, colorful, relaxed, loose, and warm. Not "sleek"—not trying too hard, just being me, Raggedy Ann.

I feel shallow writing about this, but clothes do represent us. I see how much power I have given away. Imagine the energy that looking good takes. I have a closet full of mothballs, hairballs, sweaters, dresses, jeans, and tops, yet little of it is who I really am. I only wear a few things in my closet.

I sometimes wear leather, but I don't believe in harming animals. I admit it: it's supposed to look sexy. Is this my need to be wanted? Am I going along with the media to feel cool? I'm going against my values to not harm animals. How can I make a difference in the world while caring so much what other people think?

The truth coming out of this hairball is I just want to relax, be comfortable, and feel free to be me.

I love the sweatshirt I've worn for ten years that really isn't my color. In the end, I always prefer my baggy jeans and cowboy boots.

Even underneath it all, I like my undergarments soft and two sizes larger so they don't get stuck in my behind when I bend over. I love my big panties with the stars on them.

I'm gonna put on my flannel pajamas, my terry cloth robe with the teddy bear on the back, and my fuzzy, leopard slippers.

## HAIRBALLS FOR THE READER

Are the things you're looking for in life in tune with who you are and what you value?

How would you describe your authentic personal style?

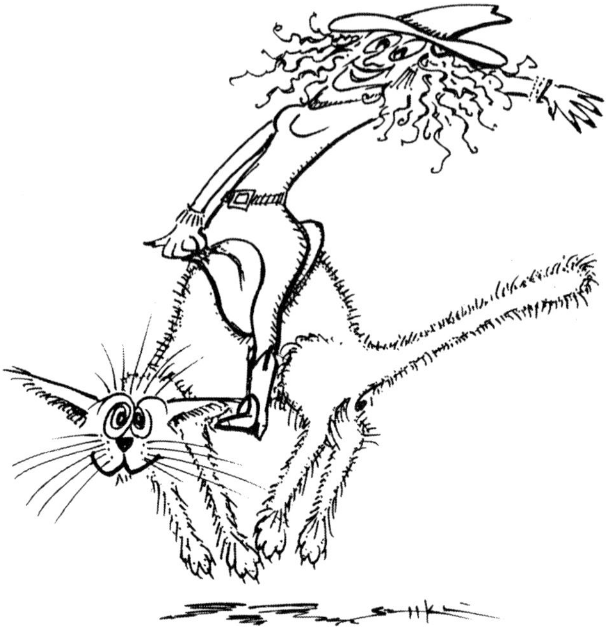

# Wild Woman Blahs
## Letting My Light Shine

*I imagine one of the reasons people cling to their hates so stubbornly is because they sense, once hate is gone, they will be forced to deal with pain.*

A James Baldwin quote from John Amodeo's book *Love and Betrayal*

I'm frustrated, chomping at the bit. Why do I feel so flat, afraid to speak, scream, cry out to the world about what matters to me most? I want desperately to experiment, try things, risk, and make mistakes. I want to find out what I like and don't like so I can see who I am. I never felt I could do these things because the need for approval stopped me. And now that I'm self-expressive, I fall down more, like a kid learning to roller skate.

I went to choir practice tonight thinking, "Oh what fun, I love to sing." But it was hard. I hated it. I couldn't find my voice. I couldn't harmonize. The guy next to me kept putting his finger in his ear. His mouth puckered like he had just eaten a lemon. I sang more quietly, sounding like a wounded bird. I wondered, is this my discipline problem? Am I an old dog who can't learn new tricks or is singing just not my thing?

Or maybe choir just isn't my thing. Sometimes I overanalyze things when I just need to accept reality. Trying and failing is no fun, but that's how I learn. Why am I so fearful of trusting my own truth, listening to my intuition, going with the next audacious or creative idea? Until I learn to stand in the fire, risking rejection or disappointment, I'll remain a dull thud: the damper over my own flame.

I'm happiest when I have my authentic pain and my excitement. My last boyfriend was a mirror of me, a rumbling, wrestling Rambo. His wildness was what attracted me to him, but it was too much. I often wanted him to calm down, though at the same time I was yearning to be more alive, to live my whole self.

That relationship made me realize maybe I need to own my own vibrant, outspoken self instead of stifling it in other people or asking them to express it for me. I've got to go beyond my fear of fitting in. He and I had so much fun! His audacity gave me permission to be a bright light! My stallion is still in the stall; it's the wild hair in me, and it's a hairball.

## HAIRBALLS FOR THE READER

How often do you take risks or try new things? What could you try?

Do you ever feel afraid of following a whim? Why?

What lights your fire?

What's something you've always wanted to do, but never have? Why haven't you done it yet?

# Too Much Baggage
## Living Simply

*You can only be as authentic as you are self aware.*
Susan Campbell, Ph.D.
*Getting Real*

I walk into the store looking for a purse, driven to find just the right one, the one that holds everything, the bag that reflects who I am or who I want to be.

Why is this subject important? Why do we carry too much baggage? Are purses, luggage, laptops, backpacks a reflection of our artificial lives? So, I go shopping for a new purse this week. The store is full of magic, my heart races. The red purse with a thousand pockets pulls me to stand in front of the mirror. I have pizzazz. I examine the insides as if exploring a cave for the first time. Pockets, zippers, little inserts for a cell phone. Wait, does it go with anything? Will it reflect poorly on me in professional settings? I mean, red with a blue suit? Fear overcomes me, yet I want to have fun.

There are also more practical purses: big clunky bags with huge bottoms, with openings like black crevasses into which you could disappear and never find yourself again. Am I carrying too much on my shoulders? These purses are like deep pits with no bottom. My back hurts. Am I carrying the weight of the world, trying to do too much? Who cares about this whole subject? Women do because we know we're burdened. Even the men I know carry packs or two wallets.

I see black purses, huge carry-on bags with roller wheels (who has that much stuff?), backpack purses (for hard-working types) and shiny purple purses, paired with gloves (this has gotta be for the sophisticated person). If only I could be together like that.

Tiny purses are cute; I guess petite is in. They make you want to squish them and "ooh." The sequined ones are darling; the little square ones are miniature boxes; the velvet ones beckon your touch. There's always a minute when I believe that I can be this woman with the purse that exactly matches my outfit, the little bag dangling as I whirl in my flowing dress.

But my stuff, my responsibilities—two sets of glasses, a heavy wallet with ID of every kind, hankies, keys for doors and cars, three different lipsticks, and pens—do not fit in a tiny, cute purse. I'm just not a fairy princess. I have to manage everything, and I need my "tools" to do it.

My new boyfriend stands beside me at the counter. As my cell phone rings, I need to write myself a note and

I reach into my purse for a pen. He wonders, "How disorganized can she be?" There I go, reaching, poking, stroking, struggling, juggling, and still no pen.

Back to shopping. On the other hand, I do look sweet holding the petite purse with the black sequins that holds one lipstick with no room for money or glasses. And with the sleek black dress and pearls, I sure would look put-together for that one night. Bent from confusion, scratching my scalp, I lean over the counter and ask the clerk, "How do women do this? These small purses are so sweet, but I always end up without something like eyeglasses, breath mints, or tampons." She says, "Those women are probably really organized."

What's going on? Am I looking for something to contain my life? I have a fundamental need to grab onto something that sustains me, something that's reliable.

Baggage is a reflection of something deep about who I am. Do I feel secure in the world? Can I reach down and find the things I need to support my life? Or am I stuffing part of myself into too-small, too-dark compartments?

Who am I really? A rhinestone cowgirl, a petite pink thing, a strong businesswoman with expensive leather off the back of a poor cow, or a practical, natural fiber, hemp-carrying feminist? It makes me wonder who's holding the purse strings.

I think I'm struggling to get rid of all the "shoulds" I've been carrying.

So, I leave the store after buying the large bag with a huge photo of Las Vegas on both sides. What's up with that? I mean it's not at all the type of purse one would carry to a professional job. But it reflects a fun-loving, let's-enjoy-life-while-we-can part of me that I renounced much too early.

This offbeat purse says to me, "I can be different, playful, and audacious." The need to be responsible often outweighs my sense of fun. I don't want to let conformity steal my creativity.

I think I'll go back and get that tiny pink bag, the one with the feathers on it. What the heck! There's an angel in me, too, buried just under the devil in the blue dress.

## HAIRBALLS FOR THE READER

Do you dress like yourself, or are you being influenced by some internalized fashion edicts?

In life, do you try to please others rather than go by your own standards?

In which ways do you feel burdened, both by physical and emotional obligations? What would make you feel more light and alive?

# Dance to the Music
## Express Yourself

*After silence, that which comes nearest to expressing the inexpressible is music.*

Aldous Huxley
*Music at Night and Other Essays*

For me, music, flirting, and food are the best things in life (right up there with animals and nature). In this world, where freedom of expression is often limited, at least we can sing or dance! But, lately I've been wondering why it's so hard to keep more of the melody—and the magic—in my life. And, there are so few places to go dancing unless you stay up late at night or take lessons. To me, that's like going to school to learn about sex.

Like, the other night, I finally got out to frolic and boogie. The guys were all lined up with their backs to the dance floor while the women danced with each other. What's up with that? I mean I enjoy women. But, as I waited for a guy to ask me, my mind was already halfway home and in my flannel pajamas. I slumped out to the car and later ended up lying passively in bed with my popcorn, watching somebody else rock and roll to loud music on TV. I lay there thinking, *How weird! I go out dancing, the guys are too shy to dance, and I end up lying flat watching movie stars doing it.*

People seem to take dance classes now. Isn't that an oxymoron? How can I allow music to become like everything else, regulated, done properly, on schedule with restraint? Seems we have as much performance anxiety about song as we do about sex. Or, am I just undisciplined?

I'm venting here, getting my hairball out, when I'd rather be shaking my hair all over the dance floor. I'm frustrated because it seems that music, like life, has been put into a box of mass commercialism and ego. We've lost the natural quality of just doing it! I guess that's reserved for big companies like Nike. It seems spontaneity is hard to get these days.

I hate it that music belongs only to those who are disciplined, work really hard, become musical stars and earn everyone else's worship. I mean my current partner designs and builds guitars and the world falls at his feet! I guess people are in awe of someone who plays that instrument. They appear to think the guitar is God or a phallic symbol. Why do we have to be good at something to be adored?

I love music, but to enjoy it, either I have to take lessons or drive an hour so I can hear it. I'd rather shake my booty than sit on it! I'm at a desk all day at work, sit in the car to get there, then sit some more in a concert. I don't want to learn something new at the end of the day. I mean, people who do, that's great. It's lovely to watch them. But, for me, I can't stand it (or sit anymore on my bottom).

I cringe at being in a class to learn something that is fundamentally primitive. I don't want to settle for lying down, not having a voice and not being in my body.

I remember the sixties when music and poetry were everywhere. It was effortless to swirl around, dancing unashamed wherever I went. Nowadays music can seem like a job.

I want to express myself and move without guidelines. I'm tired of sitting stiffly. I'm just going to have to dance and sing when I want to, even if I'm off key and ignore funny looks from people.

Some people like to dance, "One, two, one two." Some prefer freestyle movement and floating around alone in a large room, a great way to get in touch with oneself. I have nothing against either way. I just wonder what happened to vibrating wildness and interconnection?

The other day I was looking at a lawn chair in a grocery store, wondering if I should buy it for my back deck. After all, sitting is in nowadays. A friend walked by and said, "I saw you dancing the other night." I shrunk into my chair. To my surprise he added, "I guess if people weren't afraid, that's the way they'd dance all the time." I turned red and I blurted out something apologetic like, "Yeah, I don't really know what I'm doing, I just let go." But he said, "No, it's wonderful, really."

In a world that is so full of stiffness and the pressure to be restrained, it takes courage to express oneself freely. As for me, this writing has removed the ball and chain.

## HAIRBALLS FOR READERS

Do you stop yourself from self-expression because of what others think?

How would you like to be freer?

# Chapter Seven

## Culture Clash

# Scratching Our Hairballs
## Socializing

*Profound things happen when two people sit face to face and openly explore their feelings toward each other in the present.*

Susan Campbell, Ph.D.
*Getting Real*

Where is everybody? We're all so busy. On airplanes, at work, picking up the kids? Calling home on the cell because they can't be there anymore? At home trying to become a better parent, guitarist, Spanish speaker? Asleep with depression? Flying off to see a new place or to visit parents? What's going on? Tired from too much stress, too many activities? Not answering their phones because they're doing something else?

I went to an art fair recently and watched the faces of people passing by. Families wandered around, some happy to be out, some staring at the art blankly with glazed looks. Some schmoozing went on, in between the "I gotta go" comments. One old friend said they're moving to Oregon, cheaper real estate, tired of working so hard. Most of the conversations were about relocating or wondering what's going to happen next with money, the kids, parents, housing, jobs. Why are we not connecting more in community? Are we all moving fast out of fear?

Like the other weekend, I went to the car wash because I thought cleaning the car would be an easy way to feel I'd accomplished something. I ended up running into everyone I knew. Not to mention, along the way I found a stray dog, put the hairy old pet in my back seat, picked up my cell and called the number on his collar, while driving!

Are we all running around? Few of us attend city council meetings or belong to groups that help create change. Most of us are trying to take care of day-to-day details but rarely get together to talk about how to shift the way things are. Today, sitting in a coffee shop, I counted twenty cell phones coming and going, ringing, but no long conversions.

The dog owner called right back and said, "Why don't I come to the car wash, meet you and get my dog? It turned out I knew her. She'd been too busy to wash her car, so she said she might as well get in line as long as she was there to get her lost dog. I had a better time at the car wash than anywhere all weekend; what's up with that? Part of it could be that people are stuck there with down time, so they are forced to connect. That instant camaraderie can happen on trains or in doctors' waiting rooms where people have nothing else to do. Maybe the car wash is one way to have community conversation right now? (That and the supermarket.)

Are we in fight or flight syndrome? Are we all rushing about trying to find a safe nest, and is there one?

Doesn't anybody want to be where we are anymore? What if we could all stay in place and create a vision for our towns and families? Couldn't we be deliberate about change instead of running in place?

What about a town hall meeting inviting the entire community to discover, and then dialogue about, what pains us; and then create groups to find new solutions? We could all get our hairballs out together. Come on, what's really going on? Is everyone sitting back in despair or denial? Do we all think it's no use? Are we depressed and anxious? Self-sufficiency seems to be the new god; we detach instead of attaching. We meditate, go to church, play softball, practice yoga, all the while not fully engaged.

Our values are, "Be separate, your own person, have your own identity, stand on your own two feet, make money, keep busy." Maybe we're all keeping up a good front instead of having our hairballs.

Without a grassroots movement, we're pulling weeds that just keep growin' back. Why aren't more people gathering to change the health care system, the price of gas, the cost of housing? Why is it so hard to find the time to connect in community? I'd like to see the proactive thinkers of each town come together much more passionately to produce a declaration of independence, a statement of our principles and make it our legacy to the children.

Sometimes when I try to get out there to make something happen that I care about, there's an internal voice that says, "I have no energy, no time. It won't make any difference anyway." This can keep us from getting together to brainstorm, argue, and create something different.

Isn't it time we connect in community to create change?

## HAIRBALLS FOR THE READER

Do you have difficulty expressing your truth to others? Why?

What is one thing you can do that would mean making a change happen in your community?

# Home Sweet Home?

## House Maintenance or Having a Life

*As we mature as individuals, there is hope for our maturing as a nation. If living in reality becomes a norm, there can be hope for more mature responsibility in communities and government.*

Ann Wilson Schaef
*Escape from Intimacy, the Pseudo-Relationship Addictions*

I don't know why, but it seems like I'm trying to hold everything up: job, face, mood, yard, and house. Why does everything have to be up, upbeat, upscale?

Even Viagra™ is in on this. What's that about? Why does everything have to be up? Why can't I downsize, download, let down? It's time for me to let go of the pressure to be up.

We all age and die, most of us gain or lose weight, and our skin loosens. What's up with that? Do we have to be in denial to keep the American dream going?

I know I'm a narcissist caught in the wringer. When I cried about it the other night, I realized that underneath all this I feel like a little girl trying hard to be good, to keep up so I'll be loved.

It's crazy in California trying to own a home. I have no time to mow the lawn, and when the house is finally cleaned I have no energy to invite friends over. I don't have money for a cleaning lady to get the cobwebs or hairballs out. I struggle every day to pay the mortgage. Sometimes I imagine being at my front gate holding onto the bars. Am I a prisoner of my own home?

Today I hired someone to kill weeds. How strange, to harm nature in order to look good. Then I was told I need a new roof and wondered, "Why am I doing this?" Am I saving for a rainy day and hasn't the storm already hit?

I thought maybe I'd sell and get a condo, but I'm really not a condo person. I like flowers and borders and the country. I thought, "Oh well, if it means a little more freedom, I'll do it." Turns out, I can't do it. I can't sell and buy in my own town because it's too expensive. I'd end up with a bigger mortgage than I have now. Maybe "letting down" my fantasy about reality would relax me. And perhaps the down payments need to stop.

I'm well over the halfway point of my life. Gravity's set in and I'm exhausted. Tired of keeping everything up: chin, breasts, behind. You know what I mean. Do I need to get more specific? Why can't I just give in? Simplify, surrender to doing less and relax?

Today I dyed my hair, and it just seemed ridiculous looking at red when the real truth is white. I get this feeling that a lot of what I'm doing has no relationship to who I am. If I could be my truest self: I'd have white hair and cowboy boots, write weird (really honest) columns for the paper, and have a husband who adores my oddball characteristics, rather than wishing I was 30 pounds lighter.

Today I got a call from a dear friend who has ovarian cancer. She's bald now. I cried, but didn't tell her. She laughed more than I did on the phone. Life is short.

Being real has to start somewhere. I laughed, too, through my tears. Maybe the problem is pretending. Could it be that reality has to be faced? I've been taught illusions: affording, staying young, going for it. I guess we all make hard decisions about what makes us happy. Keeping it up or letting it down, which is it going to be?

Foreclosure faces me now, too, and rental prices have gone sky high. Landlords don't accept pets. What to do?

## HAIRBALLS FOR THE READER

Are there ways you feel you aren't being authentic? What stops you?

What would make you feel more spontaneous, peaceful, and free?

# Juggling Too Many Balls Hairball

*Everyone has his own point of discouragement, his own wall. What you do when you hit this wall can spell the difference between helplessness and mastery, between failure and success.*

Martin Seligman, Ph.D.
*Learned Optimism*

This pace of living with so many balls in the air is insane. How can I juggle it all: bills, calls, work, relationships, artistic urges? My hair's standing on end again.

I called my bookkeeper this morning. She said, "I almost burned my house down last night." She'd put something on the stove with the timer on but didn't hear it when it went off. By the time she got there, flames were everywhere. Then she couldn't find the fire extinguisher or remember whether to put water or whatever on top of grease. I said, "What are you supposed to use?" She said, "Baking soda." I thought, no way I would remember that while flames were flying all over.

Multi-tasking all the time is so tiring. I try to reach people by phone, and they often don't even get the message. Someone said to me last week, "Oh, nobody answers messages in LA."

Even as I write this, I hear yelling next door. I get up, praying the computer doesn't crash, and I listen. What's going on? They're either watching a ball game or having a family feud. They seem nice enough, but they also let their puppy cry all night. When I finally phoned this morning to give them some ideas about dog care, they didn't answer. This stuff always happens as I sit here writing hairballs, or maybe I just notice it more.

My life is like a messy hairdo. At least this writing is helping me to wash it all out so I can see what's going on.

Why do I do too much? Is it this cultural? Am I running in circles, away from my low self image, fears of aging or loss, too focused on getting security? It feels like a never-ending spiral—a giant screw.

Do I have so many balls in the air that I've lost track of the meaning of life? What's my goal here? Am I just going to keep the ball rolling until I drop dead?

I was so burnt this month that I bought a book on eating for my blood type, went from Kaiser to a nutritionist, and then to an iridologist. The herbs I took made me so dizzy I couldn't walk for two days. I couldn't think, let alone write hairballs.

A friend is losing his job at a church because they can't afford him anymore. His eyeballs look like they're bugging out of his head. We try to keep the ball bouncing between us as we brainstorm about it all, but it seems like we've swallowed a bowling ball instead.

My new cell phone just beeped, and I can't figure out how to work it.

It takes balls to get out of this squirrel cage. Maybe I should take a chance and relocate; after all, half of my friends are moving. They're all running for the hills, evacuating to a lower cost area in California, Hawaii, Florida or wherever. What am I waiting for? Maybe it's time to quit tossing the ball endlessly in the air.

My cat had a tiny hairball this morning and that was the end of it. He's like a lake, serene sitting next to me.

That's the simple life I want.

## HAIRBALLS FOR THE READER

How do you prioritize and decide the most important tasks of the day?

What are you running from or trying to fill up with all your activity?

Are there ways you can simplify your life?

# Living in Cars?

*We live in a time when there are so many sophisticated means for communication: email, telephone, fax, yet it is very difficult for individuals, groups, and nations to communicate with each other. We feel we can't use our words to speak and so we use bombs to communicate.*

Thich Nhat Hanh

I'm in my car so much that my back aches and my butt hurts. I feel like there's a steel plate over my heart.

I get in the car in the morning with espresso and join thousands of cars on the road. How do they all coordinate themselves like that, in and out of lanes? As I squeeze by those huge trucks, it seems like they're trying to outrun me: "gotta go, gotta go." I don't know, it doesn't seem right, living in a car.

I mean, I can comb my hair, take my vitamins, call friends, distract myself from my problems or check out different kinds of cars and people. I have everything in there: dental floss, cassette tapes, and my cell phone. Sometimes I put on my lipstick or read parts of the paper. I've even passed guys shaving in the car. In the back I keep my tennis shoes (in case I can walk), my umbrella, a blanket, protein bars, bottled water, a sweatshirt, a sunhat, and gloves, everything I need. I was riding with a friend the other day. While she was driving, she began flossing her teeth. At least she's healthy!

When I started driving to my new job, my back hurt so much I thought I'd been stuffed into a capsule, bound by restraints. Getting out of the car I'd groan as if I'd taken a plane to India. Nobody seems to work where they live anymore.

Months and years go by while I'm on the road. Cut off from trees and fish and human contact, I'm geared up, huge eyeballs focused, bobbing my head as I watch that lane, merge carefully. One wrong move is all it takes, one second and well, you know. So I grip my coffee, staring with intensity and tight back at the yellow line and rearview mirror.

There are good things about being in a car. You can meditate, listen to interesting radio or tapes, or take time to think things through. You can let the mind wander. And cars are a good place to pray. Driving gives you a sense that you're keeping the ball bouncing, moving forward, not just staying in one place and stagnating.

Constant travel creates an odd treadmill, but what's scary is I'm getting used to it. I fought it for years; but at least this way I get to see scenery. I guess I've surrendered to the cultural norm; tired of fighting it by trying to be an eccentric artist and analytical thinker. I've given in to Middle America by trying to make a buck, keep up, get somewhere, and be on the move. Is this why we continue to pay high gas prices and drive so much? Are we "driven" to make a buck or just addicted to constant activity?

Living in my car keeps the ball rolling, but I still have to ask myself: where I'm going?

## HAIRBALLS FOR THE READER

Are there ways you feel your present lifestyle is a treadmill? Do you want to get off?

How would you like your pace of life to be?

What are some new positive ways you could use your car time?

# Deck the Halls With Balls

## Family Stress

*Ordinary dysfunctional families are ones that repress feelings, or families in which a parent is an alcoholic. In these families, the ability to know what you feel and to express what you feel is discouraged.*

Jean Shinoda Bolen, M.D.
*Ring of Power*

I have an idealized picture of what family holidays are supposed to be like. The contrast between my unrealistic expectations and real life makes family stuff stressful.

I feel guilty because I get ambivalent about some extended family. I often don't discuss anything important. I usually sit around trying to be nice, feeling like there's a tennis ball down my throat and a backlog of tears.

Sometimes with relatives I feel like an apple doll: tight mouth, face sucked in, body bloated, looking like a real hairball, round and grotesque. At other times, I love my family more than anyone.

What's that about? What am I afraid of? Rocking the boat? Causing conflict? What's worse, not visiting every five years or sitting on mounds of cookies and cake, waiting for the flight back home, counting the minutes, while my voice stays stuck inside?

Not being able to connect in real conversation drives me wild. Don't get me wrong, I like most of my family. It's just that it's not all "perfect." Are most families afraid to tell the truth?

I do like some of the clan and when that happens, it's a miracle. I'm just getting out my holiday hairball here on the hard parts of the deal. On the one hand, I'm learning to see the divine in everyone and trying to relate to folks who may not be just like me, but I so often split off from myself. It's like my head's floating above my body until I get back to my own house and can be me again. What's up with this? Anxiety about loss, conflict, offending, being too outspoken make me tighten. If I could just relax and be me!

I believe conversation breeds good community; so why can't I do it in my own family? I have so many fears. What if this is the last talk we ever have before someone dies, and what if it's unpleasant? What if I say the wrong thing and it's my last visit? Is it my fault, something wrong in my thinking that makes me want to explode with long-held feelings and needs? Live and let live, right? Is it really healthy, loving, or spiritual to get the hairball out in every situation? I guess I do expect too much. People are just doing the best they can.

One year Mom and Dad and I told the whole truth. Dad sobbed. I'd never seen him like that. But, soon after, things resumed the same as before. Was it worth all that honesty?

So, I tear my hair instead and sit with a lot of ice cream and cookies. I never did get it out, never said what I thought. I'm carrying a weight while also walking on eggshells; or are those eggs just tiny holiday hairballs? Are the balls on the tree a metaphor for the joy of belonging and the delicate nature of all our souls? I guess nobody wants to be hurt, everyone wants love. There are just times to hold the ball and not toss it. You have to know your positive intentions.

## HAIRBALLS FOR THE READER

Do you have unrealistic expectations about how family interactions should go?

What are they?

What would you have to shift or change in yourself to connect more fully with family?

# Giving Thanks?

## Holidays

*I experience God whenever I express my truth in the world - and that is when I have the courage to stand up and express the energy that's inside my heart... When I hold back any part of myself, I feel just the opposite.*

Article by Richard Hatch
"The Experience of God"
Edited by Jonathon Robinson

This morning I went crazy trying to get into the Thanksgiving holiday. I was filled with mixed feelings about how grateful I'm supposed to feel, when inside I'm really empty and lonely. I decided to ask my friend if we could go for a long walk and talk about God to try to give this godforsaken holiday some meaning.

I felt like I should be home with family or watching football on TV, but I've never liked holidays much.

Instead I just wanted to be in nature. My guilt and self-doubt were strong. I was surprised to hear myself saying, "I don't know why any God would love me the way I am."

Just writing about it cracks me up, literally breaks something open in my chest. I cry when I remember my mother's emphysema, our family's conflicts over religion, the longing for spirituality but settling for artificiality, the strict rules and discord in our home.

I think it was a family thing to split off from our bodies. Each in our own ways, we decided we didn't really like or approve of ourselves and that God didn't think much of us either. It didn't seem like religion allowed us to be ourselves. Whether it was masturbation or swear words, they were bad and so were we.

I've hated getting into this pain in my lungs today, but it's led me to a lot of insights. I've struggled like a bug on a rug the whole time, but I value this stream of consciousness, and it only happens if I dive deep enough.

As I was wailing, I watched myself tighten, expecting my friend to give me some kind of advice that would interfere with my delicate process. I felt really vulnerable exposing my fears about my relationship with God, and I didn't want to be judged.

If I open to what I call God, it's like a mysterious essence around me, some sort of divine light and energy that I can feel. But, having faith brings up all the times in my life that I was disappointed or traumatized. Then I close up my being, like a box. I'd rather blame others, the church or someone, than think about how confused I am (which is wild, red-headed-now-blonde, too loud, and unconventional).

I remember a sense of the divine the night my mother died. I told my partner, "something's happening to me. I cannot sleep. It's as if a weight is leaving my body." It was about 11 P.M. I recall looking at my watch, worried I was keeping him up late, being too hysterical for no reason. He did look at me sideways. I know he was wondering if I might be off the wall. I did, too. But, the next morning, they found my mother's body. The coroner said she died at 11 P.M., exactly the time my body felt as though it was lifting from the ground. My mother took her life. She was sick from emphysema. I think she missed my father. She left a note saying, "Don't feel bad. Death is natural. It is time to leave my body." I felt God pass between us that night as light filled me and tears streamed down.

I guess God is like love; it comes in odd packages, at unexpected times. I still remember Thanksgiving, a large turkey dinner, tension from political arguments, and my brother, always funny, saying "Pass the buns." It never broke the ice, but somehow we ate our way through it, or it ate us up inside.

I still don't like the idea of eating a bird. But, maybe the holidays aren't perfect. All I know is I miss my family. Now I realize we loved each other the best that we could.

## HAIRBALLS FOR THE READER

When you think of God, what do you think of?

Where did you get your ideas of God?

What gives you faith?

# Chapter Eight

## Friendship

# X Marks T+he Spot
## When Not to Speak Up

*State what is not acceptable and indicate that the cost of crossing the line will be that you will leave.*

Patrick J. Carnes, Ph.D.
*The Betrayal Bond*

In everyone's life there is at least one X. Someone you've crossed out of your life when the relationship went sideways. That's why we call them our "X," whether it's a past boss, friend, family member, or partner—they were relationships we had to stop for awhile or end completely because they felt too painful. And we're glad we did.

But how do you know when you're isolating or being too "rejection sensitive" as my therapist calls it—or finally bolting when you probably could have worked it out but were too afraid to speak up? Sad to think many relationships end because we just can't handle conflict.

Having boundaries is great, but not when we draw them too soon, without thinking.

I once X'd a girlfriend out of my life because I was in conflict with myself over my own feelings when I was around her. Recently I found the strength to call her and tell her some of the fears that I couldn't talk about before. Since then we chat from time to time, and I see that she is a great person. We both took responsibility for how the break happened, too.

Often it's extremely hard to know when to hold the line and when to fold. But, there are clues. If your gut is churning constantly, you might need to get out. When one or both are too fragile or stressed to share what you're needing or intending, there can be little resolution. What's necessary is a balance between expressing our own truth and listening respectfully to the other. This requires skill.

In some relationships, anger or anxiety is okay to talk about if it's direct and both people want to gain insight from the dialogue. But, going into the lion's den with a blamer who is not accountable for his or her own part in the problem can leave me feeling like I'm chasing my own tail. When the hairball gets too messy, it's time to stare at the rug and meditate. It's good to slow down—before you throw the glob at someone without permission.

There are ways that make working through conflict easier, like making "I" statements that own how you feel and don't blame the other person. These are not to be confused with statements such as "I feel that you are screwed up." I used to try it that way, until I realized it was another way of covering my anger with a clever shield.

The other day I did better. Instead of turning my back the way my cat does—you know how they sit right down in front of you and turn their rump to you when they're mad? I went up to my partner and said, "It's my intention to say things to you respectfully, but give me a minute to breathe." I had wanted to scream, but I said instead, "When you are so stressed that you forget and leave the house unlocked, I feel scared that we won't be safe in our home."

This may seem like an overly simple example, but small incidents tend to remind us of feelings from our past that got disowned because they were never felt. When we own our projections by expressing ourselves responsibly, "When you said this or did such and so, I felt that...." we take back a lot of the rage we've been directing both outward and inward. In *Saying What's Real,* Susan Campbell says being "careful to speak about what actually happened and not your inferences or interpretations" is key.

Ultimately, the reason communicating like this is so difficult is that most people don't enjoy being vulnerable. Anger is mostly rooted not in fury, but in a soft spot, a need for connection. Somewhere deep inside we are hurt and can't admit it because, just as when many of us were children, we don't feel safe with the person we love. We're afraid we can't live with them and we can't live without them.

Like many people, I find it easier to act angry with my partner than to say, "I'm feeling scared because I found a bad looking mole on my arm and want to lean a little before facing the doctor." Usually it's hurt or fear we don't want to admit.

If we can know our own reality, we can more easily enter conflict and navigate it. In *Getting the Love You Want,* Harville Hendrix, Ph.D. says we must practice thinking clearly and listening non-defensively if we are to evolve as a species. This way, we can develop a "new brain" that "recognizes that being criticized for burning waffles is not the same thing as being attacked with the bread knife."

Describing when to cut off relationships or responsibilities requires enormous wisdom and maturity. In *Facing Love Addiction,* Pia Mellody stresses that, instead of communicating, we fall into "trying to fix or change the other partner...or abusing the partner with so-called 'honesty,' or violations of internal boundaries."

If I am in touch with my feelings, I can decide what is enough criticism or abandonment and be more aware of how I'm being hurtful. While we're learning to communicate, to eventually be safer people to be around, sometimes what's called for is to take time-outs or even play the X card and leave. This is particularly true when one or both lack the basic intention of creating win-win solutions. As Ulanov says, ideal negotiations need: "the feeling that results from owning a secure self with stable boundaries linked with ourselves and connected to others outside."

Building connection is always what our soul wants. It's hard to say good-bye because the pain of loss arises, and this grief of parting is usually anguish we wish to avoid. But living with ourselves and finding peace in our own skin is also important. For those of us who grew up with trauma, letting go of dependencies on toxic relationships is difficult, because we are accustomed to neglect or chronic mistreatment. If your health is tentative or you continually feel unsafe, it can be best to step around a relationship hairball.

When I'm at this type of turning point, I often have two voices in my head. One says, "Try to work things out. Try harder to talk and create resolution." The other says, "I have never felt safe around this person. If he or she is consistently acting nasty, mean, and flashing big guns, it might be time to leave."

Sometimes verbal, emotional or physical abuse demands that we have enough esteem to leave. It's always ideal to find resolution. Choosing withdrawal or detachment may be necessary if we experience neglect or abuse. When you reach an X spot, you need courage in order to cross into a new way of relating. How we communicate is the difference between a violent world and a connected one. When I am most healthy, I ask for respectful listening and speaking and offer the same. But if I've done all that I can and I'm repeatedly not heard, I need to stop the conversation and the relationship.

## HAIRBALLS FOR THE READER

When have you felt safer ending a relationship because you weren't skilled enough to resolve conflict? What are your feelings about it?

When have you successfully turned a conflict into peace by being able to communicate your feelings and intentions honestly?

What skills, such as "I statements," do you need to develop so you can have more engaged and alive exchanges and more intimacy in relationships?

# Fur Flying Friendship
## Conflict in Friendships

*My friend's assertion that dialogue is as simple as chewing gum is dead wrong. Chewing gum is simple; it is both easy to understand and easy to do. Dialogue is neither easy to understand, nor easy to do.*

Daniel Yankelovich
*The Magic of Dialogue*

It's assumed that women are good at friendships. We're supposed to have a lot of them, like fuzzy rabbits, enjoying each other: happy, hopping, shopping, talking all the time. But often we don't say what's on our minds. We harbor mixed feelings and when the hairball comes out, unfortunate things are said. Then we're too sensitive, thinking that friendship should have no conflict.

This hairball I have to get out is no warm, cuddly hare. It's a flying fur-ball. For me there's always this tug:

Do I do what she wants, pick her up at the airport, have her overnight, sit with her husband, with whom I have nothing in common? Do I rush to her side when there's pain, divorce, marriage, childbirth, relocation?

It's hard to balance my life and be a good friend. If I think of myself, I'm concerned that I'll be labeled difficult, selfish, or confrontational. I'm concerned that my friends will reject me or be mad at me if I bring up my own needs. My inner voice consumes me: "Let it go, lighten up." I feel like a bad friend if I'm not always nice and giving. But, between women, nothing is ever forgotten: thoughts and feelings that stay in the gut turn to judgments.

Many of our mothers didn't teach us to talk to each other honestly as women, and they never learned to either. Kim Chernin, in *The Hungry Self,* describes some of the long held resentment females repress.

> "Generations of women who suffer guilt;... mothers who know they have failed and cannot forgive themselves for their failure; daughters... who cannot feel rage at their mother because they know how much she needs them to forgive her."

I guess we tend to either blurt things out or stuff it. But conflict is frightening, and it's no wonder I'm too scared to say "no," to tell the truth to friends, or to be different. My drive to be whole was stunted trying to negotiate my own needs in the face of my mother's. It was so hard for us to talk to each other because neither of us knew how. Deep down there was blame, each thinking it was the other's fault that love didn't flow.

Nobody ever taught us that love includes negotiating differences and listening deeply to our own needs, as well as caring about others. So, tonight, I sit alone wondering where my friends are. A few have gotten remarried, necessitating less contact; some have moved. Some are hurt because I wasn't generous enough or I said something wrong. Some want more time, while others need more space; some want to chat incessantly, while others seem indifferent about getting together. A few are traveling the world and never available. Others want more than I can give, so I beat myself up wondering if there's more I should be doing. Maybe I'm not so great at sustaining love and friendships.

Last week a friend said, "We are on different paths now." I got so anxious, I said, "Oh yeah," and suggested "letting the friendship go!" I felt hurt and confused. It's not easy to talk effectively about our relationships, especially when dealing with conflict. Being rejection sensitive, we withdraw or become angry, rather than clearly defining our agreements.

In her book, *The Hungry Self,* Chernin says women separate developmentally while trying to hold their connection to Mother. We become self-destructive through eating disorders, depression, and self-hate. We feel, says Chernin, "a sense of loss at separating from the mother and directing these feelings toward her own female flesh, the woman coming of age today involves herself in an intensified act of self-destruction at the very moment she is seeking to evolve a new sense of self."

Tonight I'm hungry and agitated. When I start getting close to women, I fear giving myself up. I often feel judged if I'm selfish, animated, or neurotic. All I ever wanted from my mom was that she become her own person and let me be; that we might have reveled in each other's independence and authentic selfhood. I never had that, but I grieve the absence of it in every piece of clothing I put on, every creative act, every success, and every published article. I wish I could have been more honest with my mother. I wish we could have rejoiced in our unique opinions and view of life. Instead, I felt I needed to be a "clone" in order to keep her calm.

I need to know that my friends love me and are honest with me and there for me. It's a teeter totter, standing on my own two feet and feeling my power without fearing jealousy, clinging, or guilt trips from friends. I dance between my need for freedom and self-expression and my craving to be understood. Talking about difficulties helps.

I want to burn my candle brightly, be passionate and real, without fearing I'm overbearing or bad. But as Chernin says in *The Hungry Self,* "There is a sleeping giant in the female psyche, a potential for great power and potency and self-expression. At present it is entangled with mother-rage, which so often for a woman ends up directed at the self."

It's time women try to work through conflict and become more supportive of each other. As women, we're ashamed of our needs, believing we're insatiable, selfish, or too dependent. At the same time, we're tired of always being strong, armored, and isolated. We fear we'll be rejected in our friendships if we spit out the ball of hair, like saying, "I feel alienated when you brag about your great life. What I'd like more is..." Or, "I feel judgmental when you always seem depressed." These are things we need to sort through with each other, unwinding the hairball like yarn, then knitting it together, working jointly to find some creative ground. Some of us resent giving, fearing we'll be further drained when we're already exhausted; some withdraw out of fear of being a burden. Many of us are still ashamed of our moods and desires. We must learn to speak to each other about our needs without making each other wrong.

We've learned to stuff our hairballs, to be envious and competitive, with our nails stuck out at each other like cats. We've been pretending we don't need each other, but we do—desperately.

## HAIRBALLS FOR THE READER

Do you hold back from expressing your true thoughts, beliefs, and desires with your women friends? Why?

Which women in your life do you most want to communicate with now?

What do you want them to know?

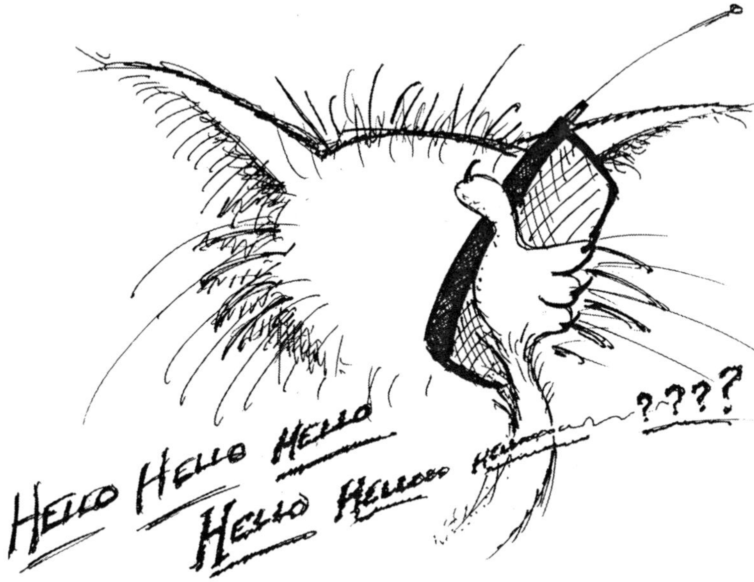


# Dropping the Ball on Friendship

## Endings

*Because of the borderline's perfectionism and tendency to perceive things in black-and-white extremes, he attempts to obliterate unpleasant feelings rather than understand or cope with them.*

Jerold Kreisman, M.D. and Hal Straus
*I Hate You, Don't Leave Me*

It's amazing how many people cut off a friendship without dialogue. You're close to someone for years and then they're gone. What's up with that? Even the people I thought were such great communicators. Why did I think they were more able to dialogue than they really were? Then there are the ex-lovers. Everything seemed so tender, so special. The talks were deep; the trust was building, then, wham, nobody's home. Where'd they go?

Looking back, these people seemed bright. Some had been in therapy, they'd read a lot, were sensitive, good listeners. They were fun, charming, giving, and there when I needed them. How could my friends just disappear?

Maybe I act rude. I can be fussy, a chatterbox, or sometimes complaining. But, how can I know what I've done if they won't tell me? Some won't return my calls or respond to e-mails. Then, when I reach a girlfriend, she says, "Oh, it's not you; I've just been busy, changed boyfriends, whatever." What's really up here? And why do other friends stick around, insist they love me, and seem devoted forever?

The books say that people who cut off relationships are "black or white thinkers." One day I'm their good friend and the next day their worst. It seems to stem from a difficult childhood where they couldn't trust their environment. Still, it's the weirdest feeling. It hurts my heart.

Not that this happens to me a lot, thank God. But the people who have disappeared were often the ones I least expected it from. Little did I dream they were afraid of confrontation, to tell me their truth. After being friends for six years, one guy apparently felt rejected because I didn't call enough. Another "good" friend, also a therapist, said she got too busy with her kids, so she quit calling. Another friend said I was rude over dinner one night. When I profusely apologized, asked that one boo-boo in six years of enjoyable friendship be forgiven, no enchilada.

The loss of a friendship, whether it's just for shopping, going to the ball game, talking twice a year or once a week or exchanging e-mails is important and tender. It's a big thing.

I can be too cowardly to tell my truth, afraid to get the hairball out, to hurt their feelings, too. Sometimes I just let people go, not meaning to or, I couldn't handle working through the differences with them. Other times I just didn't think it was possible for either of us to change enough to work it out. Was that a good excuse to help me avoid hard conversations? I ended up dropping the hairball instead of getting it out of my mouth. Sometimes we end relationships with no clarity, no completion because it's too stressful; sometimes it's a cop-out, other times not.

There's a woman in my community who drives me nuts; we always seem to bump heads. I want to run for the hills every time I see her, prove her wrong, shake her off like an apple from a tree. But in a small community or a family, it's not that easy.

I want to bridge the gap between us, but what can I do? I'm uptight around her. She seems constantly critical. It takes courage to keep telling her that I wish we could have fun together and end the strife. Finding my voice and stating my wants with her is my work to do. I tell her I want her to stop her attacks, that I feel unsafe around her. I'm a hero every time I speak up with positive intent.

What repairs a broken fence between people? Why is it so hard to simply make a phone call and say, "I wish we could heal this." It takes guts to gulp down one's pride and speak up with positive intent.

I believe boundaries can be a substitute for soul. Pushing people away or ignoring them doesn't build love. Connection comes through wrestling with conversation. If we can't learn to talk with each other, we'll just have more distance and war. But, sometimes it's just too challenging, enraging, or terrifying.

I feel so exhilarated every time I tell the truth, yet the terror of being shamed or rejected is bigger than my desire to bridge gaps for today. It's just too hard to face conflict with some people. My fear wins and I withdraw.

I'm dropping the hairball, at least for now.

## HAIRBALLS FOR THE READER

Do you use boundaries for protection when what you really want is to connect?

Talk about a time you dropped the friendship hairball. Why did you drop it? How could you pick it back up?

# Hardball

## On Judging Others

*In a way, I can understand why he stayed away—*
*his experience of home was chaos and criticism.*

Martin Friedman

*Straight Talk for Men About Marriage*

Judgments create walls. The minute I have one, there's suddenly separation. It's as though a critical thought divides the air between us and sends a possible personal connection out of the ball park. Judgments pass through my head all the time. The question is what to do with them?

I remember being on a date, having a great time and suddenly I tighten up. I feel a judgment coming on; I'm afraid I'll say the wrong thing. "Maybe the moon is in

Virgo," I think to myself. "Maybe these thoughts will fade. Please, God, I was having such a good time a minute ago. Why do I have to notice his socks have a hole in them; his wallet looks worn? And why, oh why, do I have this idea that telling the truth is a good thing?"

I hate it when this happens because I don't know what to do. I'll be at a party or a company meeting and a quick thought flits through, "That Susie so-and-so isn't my type at all. She eats meat, married a policeman, doesn't know how to spell, goes to church, doesn't go to church, wears short skirts, is arrogant —whatever."

What do I do with the hairball in my head? Is it a good idea to stuff these thoughts and pretend? Is it politically correct; a necessary part of social life; a proper way to rise to the top; the only way to succeed? What do I do with that? Why do these critical thoughts pop into my head right in the middle of conversations? No wonder we're such an isolated culture.

I can spend hours chatting at a party while a string of thoughts run amok through my mind. "He smokes cigarettes. She's always late. Is he honest? She's boring. This person is so defensive. That one talks so much, I can't get a word in. That gal is friendly, but did you hear what she did to her husband during the divorce? This woman is interesting, but spaced out. How does she get anything done? This one is fun, but what's with the hairdo? Is that a wig?" and so on. My stomach usually hurts when my mind comes up with this stuff and then my face twitches, revealing it all. My date says, "You're getting that look again." I feel as though I'm going to throw up.

Maybe that's the whole point. Is it better than stuffing? Will it ruin our evening if I say what I'm thinking? These moments make me feel strange, as though the ground between myself and the other person has suddenly become a crevasse. I used to try to be spiritual and disregard these thoughts, thinking I was becoming a better person; that maybe meditation helps. Then I considered that my judgments might be serving a purpose.

I like to get things off my chest. Speaking the truth gives me invaluable feedback. Maybe the guy with holes in his socks doesn't realize this affects his status.

The challenge is, how do I say it in a way that doesn't hurt the other person? "I enjoy your company, but could you listen more and let me do more of the talking?" Hmm, that wasn't too hard. Perhaps if I cough up my feelings and thoughts more politely, I can share them with people that I'd otherwise avoid. On the other hand, maybe if I keep meditating, I'll let go of judgments.

## HAIRBALLS FOR THE READER

What's one judgmental thought that you've had about someone?

How might you have shared your opinion or your frustration to that person without hurting their feelings?

How can you work through being so critical so you can connect better in community?

# All Together Now
## Learning To Be a Friend

*To put it very bluntly, the unspoken bargain between women is that we must all stay the same.*

Luise Eichenbaum and Susie Orbach
*Between Women*

If it weren't for my friends, I'd be six feet under. They've kept me going, helped me love myself, and pleaded with me not to give up. They've given me hope by making me laugh, taking me to dinner, and helping me to feel pretty again. I can't imagine how I could have gone through the death of both parents, the loss of my dog, and a divorce without them.

But, nobody taught me Friendship 101. Over the years, maintaining community has been more difficult and sometimes paradoxically easier than I thought. My friends and I haven't always been perfectly compatible, but then, all relationships have challenges. Some people can't communicate, some are too demanding. Sometimes my sensitive nature makes me imagine alienation, while the other person just flows like a tranquil stream.

Then there's gossip. What to do with that? Sometimes I say, "Don't tell me, I can't keep secrets." At other times I love hearing all the dirt. What's with that? They say curiosity killed the cat. Why don't I stay out of it?

I've met all types: friends that were crabby, spaced out, gabby, or money borrowing. I've learned from them all, even the ones I wanted to get rid of. There were these weird and quirky folks who were sometimes fun, painted my living room for a decent price, and played guitar on my porch, but then got suddenly irritable when my mail went to their address by mistake. Go figure!

Then, there was the woman who told me I should "Get a real job!" At the time I thought, "Who do you think you are?" But because of her, I dragged myself out the door and found work. I never would have done it if she hadn't been exactly who she was and told it like it was. All these people have nourished my life. Friends are all different.

The other day, when my carpenter played heavy rock on the radio while pounding nails into my deck, I wanted to scream, "Go away!" At other times I'm so glad to come home and tell him about my day. Over the din of his hammer we chat about the aging people I work with, about elder abuse and how drained I feel. Somehow we end up laughing and arguing about who will take care of us when we're old.

I'm also a workaholic, isolating too much at my computer, always hoping that when I reach some perfect, ultimate achievement, I'll be happy and secure. What I really want is to open my front door and let more people in. Isn't it time we all thought more about how to get out of our petty little concerns? Can't we give and receive feedback with honor?

Thinking about friendships, I recently noticed a man at a dinner party who spoke about how he worked with a community service team. His story haunted me. They'd get up at 4:00 A.M. to get started. They were so committed to what they were doing, I felt envy about his meaningful endeavor and wondered why the world isn't more like this.

What I heard at that party was real conversation, an honest expression of self. It gave me hope and reminded me how, like ants, we each have our part to play. I doubt they ever return to their anthill feeling alone or disconnected after a long day of moving, lifting, and scurrying about. They simply do what's in front of them and contribute to their community.

Sometimes I wish friendship was as uncomplicated as the life of an ant.

## HAIRBALLS FOR THE READER

What are the most common problems you have in friendships?

What parts of these problems do you create or enable?

What is one change you can make?

How do you contribute to your community?

# Chapter Nine

## Change and Letting Go

# Timebomb Hairball
## Loss and Death

*Your way of life has so little to do with what you feel and love in the world but because of the many demands on you and responsibilities you have, you feel helpless to gather yourself; you are dragged in so many directions away from true belonging.*

John O'Donohue
*Eternal Echoes*

For some there are decisions about when to die, but for others it happens unexpectedly. I suppose when it's possible, each being deserves to choose, especially when suffering is too great to bear. I know there is a lot of talk lately about whether we should have the right to die.

What I really know for sure is that losing those I love is hard. I don't like to think about the fact that we all die. But my friend Ted died tonight, and though I'd only known him a couple of months, I feel horrible. I don't care about any of my usual stuff right now. Bam, it's as if a hardball has hit my chest. Why rush around and struggle all day when death comes so suddenly?

This is so difficult to write about. I can't express myself. Usually I can say what's on my mind, but tonight I can't breathe. Everything I care about seems in question.

I guess I just want to make sure I'm doing what really matters to me. Do I want to go back to my art? Or sell my house so I can quit grasping?

I feel heavy, my back bent all the way to the ground like a rainbow's arch, my hair flat and lifeless. I feel ugly as I look in the mirror. I'm a hundred years old at 57.

I'm not really sure why Ted's death has made living feel so empty. I keep asking myself, "Why do I feel this way when I hardly knew this man?" I answer that it was his sweetness, his complete reliability, his constant desire to be there for me when I needed something, and his sincerity. He was my computer tutor, but this loss seems like much more than that.

What's this about? My heart is heavy in my chest, like concrete. And my feet feel like bricks.

I wish I could cling to someone and hold on tight, but I feel like the monkey in the experiment. The monkeys never had a warm mother to hug, so they'd snuggle up to a stuffed sock. Then they were studied. They took the warmest thing it could grasp. That's how I feel.

It's not death that scares me; it's life that does.

Ted lived alone, and he didn't care much for his job. He was devastated that his cat had died a month ago. But, these aren't the reasons I'm upset. I think it's because Ted was so kind. When I'd call him about computer problems, he walked me through them so patiently. Seems macabre, that a machine is what connected us.

What a delightful person he was. Whatever my problem, Ted would offer all kinds of helpful suggestions. He was honest, I trusted him, and he laughed easily.

I was one of the last people to see him before he died. I had no idea. I came home from vacation and called the cleaning lady he'd suggested. In a language I didn't understand, she told me she was so upset, Ted had died and she didn't know why.

It's shocking, and strange to me that the last time I saw Ted, he was just hours from his death. It was last week. I ran into him at the market, toward the end of his workday, and after chatting, he said to me, "I'm outa here."

I drove for about an hour thinking about what he said. I kept thinking about the passion of his comment, "I'm outa here." At the time, I thought he was overjoyed to go home for the holiday. Still, I ruminated on this phrase. I know that feeling of being done for the day, or gone for the weekend to relax and play. He looked happy.

But, I couldn't get his words out of my head, "I'm outa here." I kept thinking about it. I don't know why. For some reason, those words hit me deeply, even days before I heard about his death. It's possible I sensed something. Maybe he did, too.

In his wonderful book about creativity, entitled *Orbiting the Giant Hairball,* Gordon MacKenzie says, "If you go to your grave without painting your masterpiece, it will not get painted. No one else can paint it. Only you."

So here I am wondering what I want to do with myself, my life, the time I have left before a time bomb comes. I want more out of life before it's over. Thank

God for my hairballs. I'm going to write more about my wild wishes. I'm not sure exactly how I want to play out the remainder, but I do know I don't want them to tack my "to do" list on my grave when I go.

## HAIRBALLS FOR THE READER

Remembering those who have died, do you have regrets or things you would do differently in your present relationships?

If you were to die unexpectedly tomorrow, would you be glad about how you've used the days of your life?

What wishes still need to be fulfilled?

# HALF PACKED AND READY TO GO

## Moving in Together

*This is a revolutionary view of marriage: that rather than leaving it to find yourself, you find yourself through it. Marriage itself is in essence therapy and your partner's needs chart your path to psychological and spiritual wholeness.*

Harville Hendrix, Ph.D.
*Getting the Love You Want*

Relocation makes me highly agitated. Every item I pack makes my hair stand on its frizzy end. I see dirt in places I never imagined before. I glare at grey-looking walls with big holes where the paintings used to be. I see bushes that need pruning, bugs under leaves, and five cats reluctant to alter their present routines.

Dust and memories everywhere, like the drawer containing the hammer and nails, string and screws, the bathroom cupboard that never came clean, the box of spare checks and manila envelopes. I feel as if I am nine months pregnant and just want it over. I try to imagine where I will put things in my new house. Not to mention how in the world I will live with a partner.

Being under my roof with another human being all the time makes me wonder how I'll condition my hair or deal with gas after Mexican food. On the phone tonight, he told me how nice it will be to have dinner together. When I guffawed, he said he didn't mind doing the cooking.

I can't breathe. I'm scared, like a caged lion. I hate meals. I like my chips at the computer with the cat. It gives me great pleasure not to cook.

Einstein and I love sitting at my desk together (he on top of the computer), chewing, picking, playing with food, nibbling through the night. I write, eat some broccoli, make a phone call, grab popcorn, and do the laundry. I like it that way. It's a single life.

Tonight, sitting here with my taco chips, the cats at their bowls, I see dust balls all over the rug. It's kind of relaxing to live alone.

Standing around half-packed boxes, I see my entire life; in one gulp I feel the years behind me and the risks ahead. I remember loves that failed and marriages that ended, photos of my parents, my brother, and the dog. Something howls in me. I want them back, to hold my hand. I don't know what to do with all the old photographs. They tell me to move on, but I want to hold them close. I'm at the tail end of packing, and it's time to let go of the past and move on.

I didn't mean for this hairball to be sad, but I miss my mother, even with all of the things she did that pained me. I miss my dad, more than words can say. I guess life is constantly moving and relocating. Was I never prepared for life's losses and changes?

My cat stares at me as if to say, "Hey, change is good. Relax, adapt, like I do."

## HAIRBALLS FOR THE READER

What makes change more challenging? What makes it easier for you?

What's the hardest thing for you to leave behind when you move?

# Blue Balls Hairball

## On Despair

*Ducking our disturbing beliefs can be good first aid, but a deeper, more lasting remedy is to dispute them.*

Martin Seligman, Ph.D.
*Learned Optimism*

I'm down today, unable to express myself. I feel like curling up in a ball instead of keeping the ball rolling. I can't even get in touch with my feelings. My hairball is stuck inside, like a bowling ball. I'm trying to have fun with this writing, but I feel blue and want to get it out. I'm angry about giving up my power, my voice, and my needs; I'm enraged that disapproval can still make me give up what really matters to me. How can I be a hot woman with so much to say and either blow up or give up and hide under a rock? What's up with that?

Never having been taught to go for what we want, do we fail to persevere? Do men persist in their goals more easily?

I shut down when I feel rejected. Despair takes over, and in my mind nothing goes my way. I decide I must accept my life as it is with few expectations. I try not to want anymore. I'm afraid to make wrong decisions or foolish choices in people, places, and things. Terrified of abandonment, betrayal or blame, of promises and plans that don't happen; instead of disappointment, I drop the ball.

It's sometimes like moving through molasses to like myself again. The other day I just couldn't go jogging. I felt heavy and wanted to lie on the couch. Then I remembered this fatigue always comes over me when my inner tyrant says, "Who do you think you are? Why bother?" I jumped up and spoke to my inner critic. "Leave me alone. I feel better after I move around." I see why some people have stopped voting and why the world is such a messy hairball. People have given up because they feel they don't make a difference. I feel flat sometimes, not the fireball I could be. I numb out, watching warily like a wolf, careful that I don't mislead myself into thinking people are something they're not. I watch too much TV. I'm depressed, afraid to admit how tender I feel. I find comfort in May Sarton's saying, "It is as if I feel devalued and abandoned at the center of my being. I sometimes feel that everyone else manages to grow up and harden in the right way to survive, where I have remained a terribly vulnerable infant."

Buried beneath my cool veneer is a puppy dog that just wants to play and be loved. But, when I'm rejected, any semblance of neglect reminds me of decades of inconsistent reward, and I give up. I don't seem to have what it takes to sustain the soul of my wishes. I can't hold the torch, putting it down after a few bumps and lumps. I do not believe in magic or miracles or my ability to create what I want. I retire from risk. Making another mistake creates fear, so I curl up, holding in my hairball.

When the inner child was not loved enough, even slight disappointments can send us to sleep on the couch or to act out in toxic or unsafe situations. Having the blues is not popular. Hiding away in this state is common. Being happy is most acceptable. Why is despair so taboo? What would I say if I could really get it out? I'd ask, "Where is everybody? Why don't we have places in this culture to grieve? Why is it so hard to tell people how scared and hurt I am? Why do I feel shame and failure when I can't balance my checkbook, lose a relationship, become ill, or I can't fit into my jeans?"

That's why I call my writings and workshops "The Courage to Speak Up:" I'm getting it out for my own health. It gives me energy to hear myself. I feel better now. The things unsaid had formed something inside me that held me down like a ball and chain. If I stuff my thoughts, they become distorted stories. Now I believe in myself again.

Okay, I feel better. I don't have to bury myself under a blanket and believe I'm unworthy when I feel hurt. Negative experiences don't have to stop me from keeping the ball rolling. Women especially have been held down too long. Sometimes it takes talking or writing about feeling overwhelmed to get me to realize I do have power and resilience. I'm going to use it to keep that old ball—the world—going in a direction that serves me, my community, and the children who follow. I want the world ball to keep spinning on its axis.

## HAIRBALLS FOR THE READER

Do you give up too easily and drop the ball on the things you care about? Why?

What will help you be more resilient when disappointment occurs?

What unspoken feelings and thoughts do you want to express now?

# LETTING GO
## Having Faith

*Love is what we were born with. Fear is what we learn. The spiritual journey is the unlearning of fear and the acceptance of love back into our hearts.*

Marianne Williamson
*A Return to Love*

It's 3:00 A.M. and I'm lying awake in bed thinking about faith. I recall what it felt like learning to ski: I had to take a chance, let go and lean into the hill or I'd be left standing like a frozen statue on the cold mountain. I'd float down the slope, skimming the white snow. It was a spiritual connection, and it required nothing more or less than faith.

I find faith the hardest when things go wrong. But, I'm learning that even pain and loss have some greater meaning. In *Beyond Ourselves,* Catherine Marshall is constant in articulating such sayings as, "Perhaps one reason that the real meaning of faith eludes us personally for so many years was that it is so simple, so practical. Faith in God is simply trusting Him enough to step out on that trust."

It's the same nowadays. Any serenity I experience is usually preceded by fear. For me, faith is like pushing a ball up a steep hill; I expect it to inevitably roll right down again. I don't trust myself either, and so decisions are difficult. I'll think of changing and then tell myself I don't deserve better. I want to make money by buying a second home or selling the one I have. I'm too scared, however, to leave my friends and take a risk.

I don't think confusion is caused by menopause or a serotonin imbalance. I think it's the accumulation of years of inability to trust, which ends in complete exhaustion. I ask myself, "What am I fighting over in my head?" Maybe this is what people mean when they speak of faith or surrender.

Tonight is one of the first times I've felt really relaxed, flowing with life, a presence of something beyond myself: rolling waves of ecstasy without any sugar, caffeine, or toxic substances, a lightness that comes and goes. My body swoons with deep relief. I'm wondering, "What is this?" Do I have an inner ear infection or have I been taken over by some extraterrestrial doing secret experiments with my central nervous system?

Believing that everything happens for a reason and relaxing is new for me. Hendrix and Hunt say in *Receiving Love,* "If one or both partners can't receive in a relationship, the healthy give and take that defines true connections is jammed and breaks down." I think letting go of rigidity is hard for me. It's always been difficult for me to say, "Let go and let God."

I wish I could feel faith twenty-four hours a day. My therapist says I was vigilant as a kid, and I have to constantly remind my inner child to relax.

When it's present, the lightness is a balm. The joy that accompanies these new-found moments of peace has taken me by surprise. Because I didn't grow up trusting, I only felt anger, strife, and trauma. For me, I have to focus on faith; it's a discipline, to get my cerebral cortex to be quiet and my heart to open and be willing to give and receive love.

Illumination is what happens when we travel beyond the ego. Maybe this is why leaning into the hill and letting go feels so holy and light.

Perhaps that's why my father looked so beautiful when he died. I remember when the doctor told him he had cancer at the age of 79. Dad breathed a deep sigh. It was one of those moments I'll never forget. It was rare for me to be invited to join with him and his physician. He looked back at the doctor and simply said, "I've had my life." He put his shirt on and walked with dignity down the hall. He had let go of all his worries and suffering; he was radiant.

Sometimes words fail. In the end, it takes faith for us to make changes and have breakthroughs in our lives.

Leaning into the hill and letting go feels good tonight.

## HAIRBALLS FOR THE READER

What does faith mean for you?

What blocks you from going on faith and trust?

Who are the people you trust? Who do you know that lives truly spiritual lives? Why?

# Chapter Ten

## The Future

# ALL OUR CHILDREN

## Passing the Ball

*The first step to take is to become aware that love is an art, just as living is an art.*

Erich Fromm
*The Art of Loving*

In the middle of my life, as I look at the world, I'm wondering, "If we can send people to the moon, why can't we find good homes for children?" How do we help them have a voice?

If the young ones of the world were all loved, educated and cared for, we'd have a transformed world. Why do we spend billions of dollars on warfare, but so little on child welfare? Where's the money for health care, foster homes, adoptions? Why in a world with so much wealth, must children suffer?

Foster parenting is a solution, but it needs more quality care and financing. At a public fair recently, I was working at an adoption care booth when a five-year-old girl came over to me, her eyes wide. She said, "I'm a foster child."

I thought, "What do I say to that?" Maybe this was too tender or intrusive for me to get into.

Then, her mother appeared, very bright and bouncy, looking proud. She took her little girl's ponytail, smiled and said, "Yes, she was a foster child, but now I've adopted her."

The little girl said, "My mom had five kids. It was too much for her."

My mouth fell open. I wasn't used to such a small child explaining why her mom left her. I asked the mother standing there, "How did you find such a precious girl?"

She said, "Oh, they told me this was going to be a difficult child. They said I'd have lots of problems, like anger, rebellion, and depression. It's been anything but." She looked at her little girl, twirling her ponytail tenderly. "We have a great time together, don't we?" They chuckled and walked away.

I know this story isn't typical, but I'll just never forget this experience. As hard as my work in foster care has been, these are the moments that sustain me.

I wondered if it was this woman's warmth and willingness to be a parent that brought her such joy. Was it dedication and hard work that brought her this darling daughter? She seemed so clear that was what she wanted. She's even a single parent. There's a mystery to life. I know she had intention on helping children; perhaps that is why she was blessed. I don't know.

My friends have been having trouble with their teenagers this past month: one ran away, and another almost died. I found myself acting strangely and going into grief over it, eating cookies and getting impatient when people didn't keep their appointments. I so want a different world, one with places where children can talk, share, and be supported on the corner of every block.

Everyone I know is struggling with their home lives or their kids. How could it be that millions of us lack child care or help with mental health or money for education and all the while the media's feeding us artificial images to strive for? Watching kids starve themselves to death from anorexia, wandering from violent TV and video games to computer programs without any human warmth, how can this be?

I worked in the field of foster care for children, and there aren't enough homes for all the children who need them. The ones that are in existence are trying to stand on one leg. How can we help families and kids risk saying what's true?

Why don't we provide safe places for kids to get their hairballs out, so they don't have to feel ashamed of their wounds? How is a person to feel loved in such a busy world? How can you cry or seek comfort? What's going on here?

I remember high school. I hated walking into the lunchroom, because I felt like everyone was staring at my body. It was really traumatic. And after school, it was scary to return home to parents who seemed confused about what they were doing in their own lives.

We'd all feel a lot more together if we lived more as a community. It really is the delicate web that holds us together. Sometimes I feel like I've fallen and I'm dangling and if I can just find some support, my little thread can be rewoven.

As I write, the puppy next door is howling because his owner left for the day. I've been telling him through the window, "It's okay, hon," and he's beginning to calm down. Is that how I felt too often as a kid? No place to let my hair down, to be heard? Animals need our voices, too.

We need to let kids vent their frustrations, throw their hairballs around, and get out their self-doubts. How can they find support for their deepest longings, when they don't feel at home with us?

Parents aren't able to help their kids feel supported, when they can't get their hairballs out themselves. They're overwhelmed dealing with sex, love, money, the house, the car, their health, working too much and holding everything together.

Arnold Mindell says in *Sitting In the Fire:*

> "Healing ourselves and our communities requires a wailing wall...where feelings can be expressed, people can weep, people can rage, and where we can be channels for each other."

They say children ask the world of us. Shouldn't they?

## HAIRBALLS FOR THE READER

What ways do you contribute to and participate in the lives of children?

As a child, who most provided you with a feeling of home? How did they do that?

What else would you be willing to do to help a child feel at home in your community?

# The War at Home
## Empowering Community

*How do you know if you're making a request--or a demand? Here's a test: How willing are you to let go of getting your need met by a specific person? A request conveys that I value both my needs and yours.*

Sylvia Hasvitz
"Enemy Images"
*Healing Our Planet, Healing Ourselves*
edited by Dawson Church and G. Genreau

Conflict in community is a given. But, we need to have more conversations that cultivate inclusion.

Recently I invited a small group of local people to join me in creating a vision for our town as a model civic community. I believe that with deeply felt principles and a mission, we have a unique opportunity to leave a different legacy for our children. To do this, it's essential we find a way to dialogue and work through problems, even when anger occurs.

Theoretical physicist David Bohm validates this while saying: "Love will go away if we can't communicate and share meaning....The question is really: do you see the necessity of this process? That's the key question. If you see that it is absolutely necessary, then you have to do something."

My vision is to see proactive thinkers join to create a declaration of independence. This declaration would be something written and left for our children and other towns, stating principles upon which a thriving community is based.

We'd encourage community members to decide on these values. Take, for example, the idea that gossip separates people. The principle would be something like: since gossip stems from fear and ignorance, we instead value direct conversation with each other. By holding the intention of safety and respect, we'd create a container in which all could be heard.

For me, the imperative of listening respectfully comes from a resounding need rooted in my family experience. After the death of both my parents, it became painfully clear the need to talk was deep inside us, but we didn't know how to speak and listen to each other. This loss lives in my body.

I want to see a town and a world where rich, poor, all colors, and all genders can sit and listen to each other with respect for the differences. As Angeles Arien says in *The Fabric of the Future,* "There are a thousand ways to go home again; there are a thousand ways to kneel and kiss the ground; a thousand ways to reconnect to the creative fire of our life dream." I'm sad about the division of economic classes, and I fear more conflict if we don't learn from and listen to each other. How can we all, from teens to adults, corporate moguls to artists, reason things out without separating into judgmental camps?

I was surprised by the phone calls I got from people the other night after a meeting. Each one was burning with some upset or history with another one. When I said, "Why don't you just call him and talk directly about it," there was a long pause at the other end of the phone. What's this about? Could it be that people are really that afraid of talking to each other? Like a beehive, we speak behind each others' backs, creating more separation. My wildest wish is that we create something new, a safe place that fosters truth and compassion.

The ultimate challenge is not so much who moves in or out of our town or whether we build or stop growth. The bigger questions are what vision do we have for our community, and what are the principles we choose to sustain us? Otherwise, our town's body, just like a human body, will continue to feel the pain we try to hide.

Our struggles are valid; we're human. But, what's the cure? What our children need from us is a new paradigm, a life of fairness and open conversation, generosity of spirit and curiosity, not hatred or threats. Must we create crisis in our community in order to come together?

## HAIRBALLS FOR THE READER

What could you do to improve your connection in community?

What vision do you have of an ideal community?

What are you willing to do about it?

## Conversations in Community
## The Importance of Neighbors

*The power of an aroused public is unbeatable. Vietnam and Watergate proved that. It must be demonstrated again....There is no cause for pessimism. For already I have seen great obstacles surmounted. Nor need we be afraid, for I have seen democracy work.*

Dr. Helen Caldicott, quoted from
*The Hundredth Monkey* by Ken Keyes

What keeps us from drawing closer in community? What kind of world makes us too busy to visit our neighbors? Do we judge the people next door, wondering if they're too loud, nosy, needy, religious, or not religious enough? Or maybe we're too tired to bother with "neighbor-hood." Couldn't we walk across the street with some chicken soup? What kind of community prefers isolation over direct conversation?

I think some minor changes in our behaviors could transform our towns. If each of us did just one thing for our neighborhoods, it could have a ripple effect and influence others to do the same. In *The Hundredth Monkey,* Ken Keyes, Jr. shows that one person or one monkey could change an entire environment.

What kind of world do we live in when work is more important than friendship? Nobody comes out after 8:00 P.M. in my town. Where is everybody? Happily married? Sleeping because their jobs take so much out of them? Is a big foot stepping on us and keeping us from conversation, love, and extending ourselves? Do we let big bills and life's pressure stop us from a life of meaning? Or, perhaps we're not wanting anyone to really know us. I've noticed lately that I get to know people more easily when I'm on vacation or at a festival or party. I think we're less afraid when we know we'll never see someone again.

We often make the familiar exchange, "How are you?" "Oh, just fine, fine." What kind of connection does that create? Isn't this language a part of this artificial value system? What if that person's parents are dying, an aunt has gotten cancer, or a divorce is devastating them? I think we have a "detachment disorder" in this culture. Self-sufficiency seems to be the new god. We say to ourselves, "Stay out of it; it's not my problem." But, good fences do not make good neighbors.

We meditate, go to church, play softball, do yoga, but we don't fully engage with each other. We've been told, "Be your own person; have your own identity; stand on your own two feet." Well, I feel like putting my foot down instead. Connection is power, it encourages creativity.

What's really going on here? Is it so embarrassing to let someone see us? When one false self meets another, what does that create? Two masks make theatre, not intimacy, which means "into you I see."

It takes courage to be real, instead of recoil. Are we running from ourselves until we're going, going, gone on this globe?

## HAIRBALLS FOR THE READER

How might you become more involved in your local community?

How do you remove yourself from your neighbors and other locals?

# EINSTEIN IS A GENIUS AND I'LL MISS HIS HAIRBALLS

## Let It Be

*There is nothing as strong as true gentleness. If each of us became a smidgen more gentle each day, the planet would be blessed with both the strength and compassion of the Sacred Feminine.*

Sue Patton Thoele
(A section from) *The Fabric of the Future*
Edited by M. J. Ryan

I began writing hairballs late at night when I was single and lonely. My cat, Einstein, liked to sit on top of my computer. His tail would wag in front of the screen, so I'd have to swish his tail back or forth so I could see what I was writing.

This was done with love, rarely with impatience. In fact, I noticed it was Einstein's tail that kept me going. After all, it was he that inspired me to "get it out"—the hairball I needed to release each night.

Ironically, over the years, Einstein rarely had hairballs. It was I who needed him on top of my computer. He was always there in a safe way, and writing with him made me feel as if we were moving together toward what mattered to me.

I'd always worry about him when he'd venture too near the road. He loved to sit in the very middle of my busy street and just dare the cars to stop. He seemed to think they needed to slow down, and besides that, he wanted to schmooz. Cars would stop or drive around him, and I'd worry all the time about it, but living in the country with four cats is unpredictable at times.

Einstein was unusual; he loved to ride sitting on my lap in the car. My friend Cassandra taught him this. He loved riding in her bra as a baby. Even when he had to go to the vet, he didn't mind at all. He liked people. He's way ahead of me in that way. But now, it's the night before his next vet visit, and I have to find the courage to decide if his suffering outweighs his joy in life. Einstein is sick, and we've been trying to make him well. Yet, each day he's weaker and wobbles until he falls off chairs and beds and the computer.

He's sullen and tired, yet he can eat a little. The life force is strong in all of us, but the inevitability of death is always there, looming. I know he and I will have to share hairballs, as we've never done before.

He'll need to tell me if he's suffering too much to stay in this world. The vet has tried everything possible, tests, X-rays, blood samples, and nothing helps.

I feel, for the first time in years, on an altered plane, a place that only death can take you. I sense my mother so close to me, my mom who loved animals.

Maybe it was because she was abused as a girl. Animals were the ones that seemed innocent enough for her to trust. I just know she's smack dab here in this room tonight, solid as a rock. My mom will go with Einstein to the veterinarian's office tomorrow, and she'll probably give us the courage to let go. She was a strong woman, though I know there were several times in her life when she worried that she had let go too soon. Her darling poodle was given away because of relocation, and she never got over it. She grieved the rest of her life.

I dread the longing of coming back to this house without him. Einstein's always been more than a cat to me. He's been my monolith, my metaphor, and the essence of what it's all about. We're into making a statement to the world through getting out our hairballs; we're into creating community by speaking up.

How can I say good-bye to Einstein? He was always the first one to greet the neighbors. He welcomed the stray cats and dogs and even invited the raccoons and possums to hang out. He was intent on co-community.

I had forgotten about this kind of pain. It's been twelve years since anyone I loved died. Death is so hard because you can't be mad at people for leaving. You can't break up and make up; it's just the end. I'm surprised to find myself with feelings I'd forgotten I could have.

I guess loss can be like labor pains; you have to forget sometimes in order to move on. Even though I have everything in the world I need tonight, I feel as if he is a part of my own body. I don't want to lose him.

Today, the vet was so kind in putting him to sleep, he even cried with me. He said, "I hope Einstein is finding wonderful flowers to sniff in heaven." And with a faraway look, he murmured, "I sure hope it's like that when I die."

I can only imagine that, if there is a God, I've got this godforsaken grief because it's the only thing in years that's broken down my walls. I'm not judging anybody tonight, and I'm not worried about career goals. My ego is collapsed.

I'm in awe of the people in my life who love me. I don't need a new car, to be established, or well known. I don't even want to be an artist. I simply want to sit on the beach and look at the shore. I only want to be kinder and less self-absorbed. Einstein taught me about love.

I may never again have a cat sit on top of my computer, and I will probably sit alone many nights without his tail leading me like a compass. It's also likely I'll never have a cat like Einstein again that loves to sit in the middle of the road facing fast traffic.

I remember as I hosed my garden, people would stop, steely, in their tracks and glare at me, "Your cat is in the middle of the road!" I'd just smile and say, "I know, but I've tried everything and can't get him to stop."

Then they'd look at me with this knowing and loving look, softening, letting go of the stress of driving and say, "Okay" and more slowly go on their way. Every day I thanked God for the safety of my cats. Every day Einstein would meander in a mellow way back into the house, safe and sound, eat a good meal and curl up. Each night I heaved a grateful sigh.

Einstein's had a great life: a social life, good food, and the total attention of community. Some are upset to know he is leaving this world.

The only good thing I can think of is that when I die someday, he'll be the first to greet me. Of that I'm sure, because he's a very friendly cat, loyal and true.

I'm sure my mother will be standing right beside him with a grin. She'll watch over all of us, more than ever.

I will miss you, my friend. But, our reunion will be the best.

## HAIRBALLS FOR THE READER

What person or animal in your life has most inspired you to be yourself?

What is the most important thing they gave you?

# How Do You Do It?

## Getting Out Your Hairballs

On attributes of Dialogic Communication: *"Willingness to temporarily suspend one's judgements and listen deeply"*

Doug Ross, Ph.D.
*A Tao of Dialogue*

Everyone asks, "How do I get the hairball out without hurting someone or blowing them away?" Speaking up so that you accomplish your goals is an art. The reason we've had war and fighting for so long in this world is that few know what to do with their frustrations. Fury is a force, and its fire can do harm.

If you learn to speak with clear intent, you can create a promotion at work or a dead relationship coming back to life. I'm not saying that "the hairball" always makes miracles, but it builds more than it destroys. The purpose of the hairball is to understand and be open to learn from each other. We've had war for centuries because anger floods the body before we use our brain and clear communication skills effectively.

It's simple:

1) State your intent and come from your heart.
2) Use only "I" statements. (I feel, I need, I want)
3) Say your request or wish.
4) Listen deeply and with respect to the other person or persons.

The last way to dialogue at an impasse (only with a very safe person who agrees to do it) is to agree to let "the inner child" inside both of you speak. You can keep this brief instruction in your wallet.

For example, my partner and I were stuck for several days in an old argument a while ago, and I finally suggested we let the inner kid inside of each of us talk. I felt silly trying it at midnight, but I also wanted to get some sleep and find a way to resolve the never-ending disagreements.

Immediately we both softened as he said, "I'm scared. I feel as if I'm inadequate." I said, "You must have felt that way since you were tiny." I told him what I heard and then I said, "I feel as if I've never really been loved by a man. I don't remember my dad telling me how much he liked me."

Within seconds we were both a puddle and held each other and went to sleep. This is playing softball.

You know, the work environment is like hard ball. Every day I fear I can get fired. And, sometimes the employer is tortured, too, by horrible decisions. I remember once telling my boss, just as I started feeling the veins in my neck sticking out blazing purple, that, "I'd like it if we could have conversations more often about how we are doing here, instead of these once-a-year evaluations, which makes me feel judged. Could we just have weekly dialogues and talk about what's working and not working?" I added my intent. This is an example of stating a vision and offering a solution instead of complaining. "I really like working with you, and I'd like to feel safer here and more a part of things this way."

Acts of outrage and frustration are rooted in unmet needs. Anger comes from the animal brain. We need to evolve into a civilized and creative culture. Redirected rage became bravery while ending slavery or freeing women to vote. Stating your intention and wishes is the most important part of any communication because it enables you to become sincere. "I'd like to be friends. What would that take?" or "I want to do a good job," or "I'd like to feel peaceful at home." Ideally, each person does this.

As with great leaders, passion needs to be placed in a new vision. We must evolve as a species.

## HAIRBALLS FOR THE READER

What stops you from telling the truth and stating your intent?

Name three unmet needs and wishes you'd like to communicate to important people in your life.

# Finding the Courage For the Next Generation

*Solitary chimps, like solitary people, seldom laugh, a result consistent with laughter's role as a social signal. But chimps and humans differ in the social situations in which they laugh—we humans have added something new to our still present chimp like tendencies. Adult humans laugh most during conversation."*

Robert Provine

*Laughter – A Scientific Investigation*

It is so sad when people die having not said what they need to say to each other. Family, friendships, or divorces get lost without enough connection. People go to their deathbed without finishing unspoken judgments, hurt, or love. The things we're afraid to say stays in the body.

Over the years, as I worked with clients, I noticed that whatever abusive situations they had suffered was not the cause of their greatest grief.

Their deepest pain arose from not having a caring person to walk and talk with them about what they had experienced. They never felt heard. We need respectful witnesses. We long to tell our stories, to get out our hairballs, to explain our life histories or share our joy.

Why are we all so bottled up or unable to get through conflicts? Everything stems from that little child inside us that was abandoned or neglected. That young, sensitive, innocent child within gets buried because it never had a voice. So, we can grow up mangled; raging against life, creating criminals and penal systems full of violent and/or pained people. This lack of vitality and juice is a loss.

Joy comes from the freedom to be ourselves. The part inside of us that never felt like enough is at the root of our sense of separation. Most of our attacking, shutting down or self-abusive behavior arises from this constantly reinforced sense of not being adequate. Our addictions, depression, anxiety, and isolation are all a result of not learning kindness early on. There's a dull, emotionally constipated feeling of perpetual self-judgment in most of us. As Alice Miller says in *Drama of the Gifted Child,*

> "For the majority of sensitive people, the true self remains deeply and thoroughly hidden. But how can you love something you do not know, something that has never been loved? So it is that many a gifted person lives without any notion of his or her true self."

I cannot say it enough: what we need most are honest, emotionally intimate talks, within ourselves and clarity around our intentions. It's okay to be confused or to do nothing for a while and stew; eventually even that reveals your truth.

The other day I said to my husband, "I'm conflicted. I love our house and don't want to sell. I'm attached to it for sentimental reasons, but another part of me wants to let go, so we can have a lower mortgage." Sometimes clarifying my wishes might involve wrestling with two separate needs. That's what the hairball is all about! Eventually, the truth will set you free. Sometimes it takes time.

I learned this from my parents. They were insistent on a life of meaning. They had conversations that mattered. I grew up around active discussions about social issues and their own marriage. My mother loved an argument. Sometimes I saw her as a wild stallion that could not be tamed. Our home wasn't perfect, but there was a lot of honesty. Authenticity put blood in my veins. So, now I'm passionate about passing the ball to future generations. Let's not allow their spirits to be broken.

It's full freedom of speech that's being driven out of us in this culture. The false self, pretension, and faking it is prevalent. We rarely make time for values of self-expression, art, and concern for others. Michael Lerner writes about how scared and feeble most of us feel. In *Surplus Powerlessness* he says of the system, "It depends on repressing a fundamental aspect of what it is to be human. As such it can only function through an ongoing struggle and that struggle has severe physical and emotional consequences for human beings."

He goes on, "The environment we are in is pervasively repressive; we're indoctrinated by media or economics." On a deep, cellular level, we're still animals needing to survive, so we're anxious or robotized.

In the sixties, we had connection, conversations through music, poetry, marches, festivals, news, and media. We were going to create a "different world." We talked about letting down walls. We didn't have acid reflex or tight jaw syndrome. We used our voices freely!

Since that time, therapists have become enamored with "boundaries" and "setting limits." I believe that boundaries are a substitute for soul. Setting limits has been misunderstood. When you say what you feel, fear, and desire, you don't need to push people away or avoid them. You won't kill anyone or dislike yourself. When you risk being authentic, people know what's happening; there is no sniper attack. Everything's on the table, especially when you learn to identify your deepest, most vulnerable needs and intention.

I just know that for me, having an eating disorder forced me to deal with stuffing everything. I found that speaking up changed my metabolism and got me out of depression and quicksand. I found that heat burns fat.

My voice gave me life. I realized I had been holding my breath. It was almost as if a large balloon with a big tie holding oxygen had been around my neck for years. I had lived above my body, disassociated. I couldn't stand the fear of rejection from my own critic or from others, so I hid.

I don't think there's a thing wrong with being fully oneself and expressive, for instance, like a large woman or a tiny man. Big or small is beautiful and that is one of the many ways of living we all need the freedom to enjoy. I love every size female. Forget what they tell you to be; I just started looking at what made me happy. Let's leave our kids the legacy of self-acceptance.

Our life force and our present world situation here on the big ball requires us to speak with good intentions and courage.

**"In the beginning was the word."**

## HAIRBALLS FOR THE READER

If you were fully expressive of your true self, how would you be different?

What legacy do you most want to leave to the world?

# Conclusion

In this book I let myself unfold in conversations, out loud. My cat was my mentor. No wonder I named him Einstein. As the process of writing and expressing myself evolved, I lost weight that had collected in my body from holding in so many emotions and needs.

The only way I know to get my power and to know what I feel is to talk about what is going on. As Dana Jack says *In Silencing the Self,* "Through voice, we locate ourselves in the world." She explains how we do not find our identity in isolation but from being heard. Her model about personal well being focuses on relatedness as opposed to self-sufficiency.

We, the people, can create a new world, but not separately. We need community to heal, to be heard in safety and courage no matter what the circumstances.

Freedom of speech is easier said than done. It requires resilience because we are not always met with agreement or without judgment. Ideally, an inner core of self-love helps so that we can be like a bouncing hairball. To stay in the ball game of life, not give up and keep the conversation going is the beginning of change.

It is not easy to listen well or respectfully or to speak up. I ask myself, "Should I bring it up?" or I wonder if what I have to say might be too hurtful. Sometimes I go home wondering what was really said, what did they mean, what could I have clarified or what was I thinking by saying what I said?

There are many reasons not to speak up but knowing our true intention and stating it helps clarify that. It is also very helpful to make "I" statements so as not to blame and then to state your needs. I know I have talked about all of this in the book already, but I can't help to draw a final synopsis. In other words, constructive conversations could change the world.

Speaking up can occur in tiny moments each day, in thick spaces of tension when we know what is not *being* said, but we become brave and say it, or in larger arenas when we take a deep breath and stand up for what we believe in.

No one wants to go to jail for speaking, lose a marriage, a friendship, or a job. So, what to do? We need to talk to each other more than ever before. Conversation needs to be valued. We might find answers to big questions if we hang in there together, without the constant use of machines and technology. In large groupings or small, in neighborhoods, within the United Nations and everywhere, hairballs for days. The big world ball depends on us.

But the fear of sharing is real. Shame lurks close by when I speak up. One night out with friends I mentioned the name of a book and was corrected abruptly. I had mispronounced the title. I was quiet for the rest of the evening, wrestling with my inner "bun lady" (the critic). "Did I sound silly? Was I too loud? Was my excitement out of place?"

Sometimes we're resentful, paranoid or confused. Recently with an old acquaintance, I blurted out, "I'd like to clear up our misunderstandings." That's all it took. In that one moment, we opened a new relationship and grew closer again. Inside, I heard "don't rock the boat." But, I carried my hairball down the field, taking a deep breath and it paid off.

I believe that boundaries are a substitute for soul. Often, we put up walls when we are afraid to talk to one another. The national defense is not different from our own armor. Isn't it time to drop it and do something else? Yes, there are times to say "no" and step out of harmful situations, but we also have to learn as a species to dialogue in conflict. If we are going to change a world that is full of huge hairballs, can we be proactive?

Here's where the personal becomes political. If we don't learn to deal with our differences daily and speak up for our values, will we have the power and strength to deal wisely with global issues?

Maybe you say it's not enough. The problems are too big. Or, you could argue that talking isn't going anywhere; we have to "do" something. Yes, we do. But, I believe that moving forward with vision emerges from deep dialogue. What we have not done, collectively, is come together and put our cards on the table. It is only out of brainstorming and sharing that we unify. Safety is built from the ground up as we speak "our peace."

As journalist Tom Hodgkinson says so well in *How to be Idle,* "The idler's love of chat, sadly, is demonized by a society that prizes action above all else. 'Don't talk about it - do it!' is the modern mantra. To which I reply, don't do it, talk about it. If the thing talked about is worth doing, then it will get done in its own time." I am not saying that we should talk on and on forever. It's just that hairballs do matter, embarrassing as they can be.

I often think about the way ants carry a bread crumb up a hill. Odd that insects work together better than we the people. Couldn't more conversations produce new systems, new ways of being, and create a world for the common good?

Let's please keep speaking up for the voiceless ones, the earth, the animals and children who need our words to protect them and provide for a future.

It is my contention that conversation can change the world.

# Bibliography

Amodeo, John, Ph.D. *Love and Betrayal: Broken Trust in Relationships.* Ballantine Books, NY. 1994. Baldwin, James, quote from Book of Quotations.

Bennett, Hal Zina. *Write From the Heart: Unleashing the Power of Your Creativity.* Nataraj Publishing, a Division of New World Library, 1995, 2001.

Bessel, A. VanderKolk, M.D. *Psychological Trauma.* American Psychiatric Press, Inc. Washington D.C. 1987.

Bohm, David. *Bohm: On Dialogue.* Madison Avenue, NY: Routledge Classics, 2004.

Bolen, Jean Shinoda, M.D. *Ring of Power: Symbols and Themes: Love Vs. Power in Wagners Ring Cycle* and in *Us: A Jungian Perspective.* Nicholas-Hays, Inc. York Beach, Maine, 1992.

Brockivich, Erin, with Eliot, Marc. *Take It From Me: Life's A Struggle But You Can Win.* McGraw Hill, NY, 2002.

Campbell, Susan, Ph.D. *Getting Real: 10 Truth Skills You Need to Live an Authentic Life.* H J Kramer Book, Tiburon, CA. Published in a joint venture with New World Library, Novato, CA, 2001.

Campbell, Susan, Ph.D. *Saying What's Real: 7 Keys to Authentic Communication and Relationship Success.* Tiburon, CA: H.J. Kramer Book. Publishing in a joint venture with New World Library, Novato, CA, 2005.

Carnes, Patrick, Ph.D. *The Betrayal Bond: Breaking Free of Exploitive Relationships.* Health Communications, Inc. Deerfield Beach, Florida, 1997.

Chernin, Kim, *The Hungry Self: Women, Eating and Identity.* Harper and Row Publishers, NY, 1985.

Church, Dawson, Genreau, Geralyn, Editors. *Healing Our Planets, Healing Ourselves: The Power of Change Within to Change the World.* Selection from Haskvitz, Sylvia, Enemy Images. Elite Books. Santa Rosa, CA, 2004, 2005.

Coleman, Joshua, Ph.D. *The Marriage Makeover, Finding Happiness in Imperfect Harmony.* NY, St Martins Press, 2004.

Dyer, D, Wayne, Dr. *The Power of Intention, Learning to Co-create Your World Your Way.* Hay House, Carlsbad, CA, 2004.

Eichenbaum, Luise, and Orbach, Susie. *Between Women: Love, Envy, and Competition in Women's Friendships.* Viking Penguin, NY, 1988.

Eichenbaum, Luise, and Orbach, Susie. *Understanding Women,* Basic Books, Inc., Publishers, NY, 1983.

Estes, Pinkola Clarissa, Ph.D. *Women Who Run With The Wolves: Myths and Stories of the Wild Woman Archetype.* Ballantine Books, NY, 1992.

Friedman, G. Marty. *Straight Talk for Men about Marriage: What Men Need to Know About Marriage (And What Women Need to Know about Men).* Little Moose Press, Beverly Hills, CA. 2005.

Fromm, Erich. *The Art of Loving.* Harper and Row Publishers, NY, 1956.

Goodman, Charisse. *The Invisible Woman: Confronting Weight Prejudice In America.* Gurze Books, Carlsbad, CA. 1995.

Hanh, Thich Nhat. *Calming the Fearful Mind: A Zen Response to Terrorism.* Berkeley, CA: Parallax Press, 2005.

Hay, Louise. *Every Woman's Guide to Successful Living.* Carlsbad, CA: Hay House, Inc., 1997.

Hendrix, Harville, Ph.D. *Keeping the Love You Find: A Guide for Singles.* Simon and Schuster, Pocket Books, NY, 1992.

Hendrix, Harville, Ph.D. and Helen LaKelly Hunt, Ph.D. *Receiving Love: Transform Your Relationship By Letting Yourself Be Loved.* Atria Books, NY, 2004.

Hendrix, Harville, Ph.D., *Getting The Love You Want.* Henry Holt and Company, NY, 1988.

Hite, Sherrie. *The Hite Report: A National Study of Female Sexuality.* NY: Seven Stories Press, 1976.

Huxley, Aldous. *Music at Night and Other Essays,* London, Garden City, NY. Chatto and Windus / Doubleday, Doran and Co., 1931.

Jack, Dana Crowley. *Silencing the Self: Women and Depression.* Cambridge, MA, London, England: Harvard University Press, 1991.

Keyes, Ken. *The Hundreth Monkey,* Section in quotes from Dr. Helen Caldicott, Nuclear Madness, Bantam Books, 1980.

Kreisman, Jerold, M.D. and Straus, Hal. *I Hate You, Don't Leave Me: Understanding the Borderline Personality.* NY: Avon Books, 1989.

Lerner, Michael. *Surplus Powerlessness: The Psychodynamics of Everyday Life and the Psychology of Individual and Social Transformation.* The Institute for Labor and Mental Health, Oakland, CA, 1986.

MacKenzie, Gordon. *Orbiting the Giant Hairball: A Corporate Fool's Guide to Surviving with Grace.* NY: Viking Penguin, a member of Penguin Putman, Inc., 1998.

Marshall, Catherine. *Beyond Our Selves.* Lincoln, VA: Chosen Books, 1961.

Mellody, Pia, with Miller, Wells, Andrea, and Miller, Keith, J. *Facing Love Addiction: Giving Yourself the Power to Change the Way you Love.* Harper, A Division of Harper Collins, S.F. CA, 1992.

Miller, Alice. *The Drama of the Gifted Child: The Search for the True Self.* Rev. Edition. Basic Books, A member of Perseus Book Group, NY, 1997.

Mindell, Arnold. *Sitting In the Fire, Large Group Transformations Using Conflict and Diversity.* Lao Tse Press, Portland, OR. 1995.

O 'Donohue, John. *Eternal Echoes, Celtic Reflections On Our Yearning To Belong.* Perennial, an imprint of Harper Collins Publishers, NY, 1999.

Provine, Robert R. *Laughter: A Scientific Investigation.* NY: Viking, Published by Penguin Group, 2000.

Real, Terrence. *I Don' t Want To Talk About It: Overcoming The Secret Legacy of Male Depression,* Scribner, NY, 1997.

Real, Terrence. *How Can I Get Through to You? Closing the Intimacy Gap Between Men and Women,* Simon and Schuster, NY, 2002.

Reynolds, David K. *Constructive Living.* University of Hawaii Press, Hawaii, 1984.

Robinson, Jonathan. *The Experience of God: How 40 Well Known Seekers Encounter the Sacred.* Selection by Richard Hatch. Carlsbad, CA: Hay House, Inc. Carlsbad, 1994.

Ross, Doug, Ph.D. and friends. *A Tao of Dialogue, A Manual of Dialogic Communication.* Medicine Bear Publishing, Blue Hill, ME, 1998.

Roth, Geneen. *When Food Is Love: Exploring the Relationship Between Eating and Intimacy.* NY: Plume, Published by the Penguin Group, 1992.

Roth, Geneen. *Feeding the Hungry Heart: The Experience of Compulsive Eating.* NY: Plume, Published by the Penguin Group, 1993.

Ryan, M. J. *The Fabric of The Future, Section from Thoele.* Patton Sue, pg. 137, Conari Press, Berkeley, CA, 1998. Angeles Arrien article quoted.

Sarton, May. *Recovering: A Journal.* NY, London, Canada: W.W. Norton and Company, 1980.

Scarf, Maggie. *Intimate Partners: Patterns in Love and Marriage.* NY. Ballantine Books, 1988.

Schaef, Ann Wilson. *Escape from Intimacy: Untangling the "Love" Addictions: Sex, Romance, Relationships.* SF: Harper & Row, 1989.

Seligman, Martin, E.P. Ph.D. *Learned Optimism: How To Change Your Mind and Your Life.* Pocket Books, A Division of Simon and Schuster Inc., 1990.

Sher, Barbara. *Live The Life You Love: In Ten Easy Step-By-Step Lessons.* Dell Publishing, NY, 1996.

Stettbacher, Konrad J. *Making Sense of Suffering: The Healing Confrontation with Your Own Past.* A Dutton Book, Published by Penguin, 1991.

Thoreau, Henry David. *Walking.* NY: Harper Collins Publishers, 1994.

Ulanov, Ann and Barry. *The Witch and The Clown: Two Archetypes of Human Sexuality.* Chiron Publications, Wilmette, Illinois, 1987.

VanderKolk, Bessel A., M.D. *Psychological Trauma.* Washington, DC: American Psychiatric Press, Inc. 1987.

Welwood, John, Ph.D. *Journey of The Heart: Intimate Relationship and the Path of Love.* Harper Perennial, A Division of Harper Collins, NY, 1990.

White, Kate. *9 Secrets of Women Who Get Everything They Want.* Harmony Books, NY, 1998.

Williamson, Marianne. *A Return To Love: Reflections on the Principles of A Course in Miracles,* Harper Collins Publishers, NY, 1992.

Woodman, Marion. *Addiction to Perfection: The Still Unravished Bridge: A Psychological Study, Studies in Jungian Psychology,* 12. Toronto: Inner City Books, 1982.

Yankelovich, Daniel. *The Magic of Dialogue: Transforming Conflict Into Cooperation.* Simon and Schuster, NY, 2001.

Zina Bennett, Hal. *Write From The Heart: Unleashing the Power of Your Creativity.* Nataraj Publishing, a Division of New World Library, Novato, CA, 1995, 2001.

## — To Order this Book—

To order *The Courage to Speak Up*
Contact Katy Byrne
E-mail KatyByrne@aol.com

or
LangMarc Publishing
P.O. Box 90488
Austin, TX 78709
1-800-864-1648
E-mail langmarc@booksails.com
or order on our website
www.langmarc.com

$16.95 + $3.00 shipping

***The Courage to Speak Up***
is also available on E-book

CPSIA information can be obtained at www.ICGtesting.com
Printed in the USA
BVOW020454040113

309545BV00006B/102/P

9 781880 292983